PANCAKES AND WAFFLES

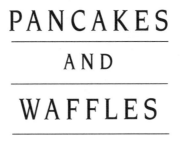

PANCAKES

AND

WAFFLES

ELIZABETH ALSTON

HarperCollins*Publishers*

HarperCollins books may be purchased for educational, business, or sales promotional use. For information, please write: Special Markets Department, Harper-Collins Publishers, Inc., 10 East 53rd Street, New York, NY 10022.

FIRST EDITION

Based on a design by Cassandra J. Pappas

Library of Congress Cataloging-in-Publication Data

Alston, Elizabeth.
Pancakes and waffles / Elizabeth Alston. — 1st ed.
    p.   cm.
  Includes index.
  ISBN 0-06-016150-7 (cloth)
  1. Pancakes, waffles, etc.   I. Title.
TX770.P34A47   1992
641.8′ 15—dc20   92-53370

93 94 95 96 97 ❖/RRD 10 9 8 7 6 5 4 3 2 1

CONTENTS

DESSERT

SYRUPS, SAUCES, AND TOPPINGS

ACKNOWLEDGMENTS

Heartfelt thanks to Ruth Cousineau; Rebecca Adams, Michael Davies, and Sandra Robishaw; Miriam Rubin; Mary Adams and Dionisia Colon; Marinella Cancio.

INTRODUCTION

Pancakes and waffles are among the most satisfying and comforting foods to eat, and the easiest to prepare. Made with the simplest ingredients—flour, eggs, and milk—they take easily to sweet or savory, and to any part of a meal, from breakfast to dessert.

A waffle is *crisp* and has a honeycomb texture from the waffle iron (or maker) that it is cooked in. Pancakes, while always *moist,* come in many guises:

- *The familiar American breakfast pancake,* 3 to 4 inches across and ¼ to ½ inch high, cooked by pouring batter onto a griddle or skillet. Start a day with a short stack of Best-Ever Pancakes, page 14, dripping with Brown Sugar Syrup, page 108.
- *A single large pancake, oven-baked* in a pie pan or other dish. This large pancake is cut in wedges to serve. Try Super-Simple Baked Pancake, page 18. It really is easy and can be used in many different ways. Baked French Pear Pancake, page 83, makes a fine dessert or brunch dish.
- *Skillet pancakes,* also cut in wedges to serve, but cooked entirely rangetop. Peter Rose's Dutch Cheese Pancake, page 46, is a good example and makes a perfect Sunday supper.
- *Unique pancakes*, without a common genealogy, made from ingredients such as noodles, corn, farina, and matzos. Try Polenta (cornmeal) Pancake with Greens and Ham,

page 53, Crisp Noodle Pancake with Stir-Fried Chicken, page 48, or, one of my favorites, Fresh Corn and Cheese Pancake, page 44.

You will also find several *crepe* recipes. A crepe is a paper-thin pancake usually 6 to 7 inches in diameter, resembling a very thin omelet. The mild taste of crepes is a good carrier for other flavors so they are often served filled. Try Black Bean–Stuffed Crepes with Fresh Tomato Salsa and Sour Cream, page 60.

INGREDIENTS

BAKING POWDER AND BAKING SODA

While both are used to leaven—a nice, old-fashioned word that means to raise or make light—they are not interchangeable. Although used as a leavening on its own, baking soda (pure sodium bicarbonate) is also used to neutralize acid ingredients such as buttermilk, yogurt, brown sugar, or molasses. Baking powder is more complex and combines acid and alkaline ingredients. When moistened, both baking soda and baking powder start to create bubbles that bake into the batter, creating light and delicious foods. Another ingredient in "double-acting" baking powder (the most common kind) acts as insurance because it only starts working when heated.

BROWN SUGAR

Although I usually specify one or the other, light and dark brown sugars can be used interchangeably in many recipes. Brown sugar is granulated sugar with a little molasses added. Because it contains more molasses, dark brown naturally gives a deeper flavor, which is sometimes not what I had in mind. But if a recipe calls for light brown and you have only dark brown in the house, go ahead and use it.

BUTTERMILK AND YOGURT

These ingredients are used to moisten flour but are also valuable for their flavor and acid content. They may be used interchangeably, although with yogurt you may need to thin the batter with a little water. Decide after you have made the first pancake.

If you don't have buttermilk or yogurt, you may acidulate regular milk instead: Put 1 tablespoon lemon juice or vinegar in a 1-cup measure and fill with regular milk to the 1-cup mark. Stir. Let stand 5 minutes, then use.

Buttermilk powder may be used instead of buttermilk. Follow the package directions.

FLOURS

The recipes have been tested with nationally available brands of all-purpose flour. Bleached or unbleached flour may be used.

When buying whole grain flours such as buckwheat or millet, look for a store that has a fast turnover and/or that keeps the less-in-demand ones under refrigeration. I buy brown rice flour only when it's kept under refrigeration, and I keep it refrigerated at home.

OILS

When vegetable oil is called for you may use corn, safflower, or any other oil with little flavor. Lots of recipes call for mild olive oil, as I found it added to the overall flavor without being noticeable as olive oil.

ACCURATE MEASURING

Although pancake batters are quite forgiving, measuring ingredients accurately will help achieve optimum results.

To measure flour, give it a couple of stirs in the bag or canister, then spoon it into metal or plastic dry-measure cups (the ones that come in nested sets).

Spoon to overflowing. Do not tap the cup on the counter or press the flour down. Draw a straight edge (metal spatula or the handle of a rubber spatula) across the top of the cup, leveling off the flour.

Use exact-size measures. If the recipe calls for ¾ cup flour, use a ½-cup measure and a ¼-cup one; don't attempt to fill a 1-cup measure three quarters full.

To measure granulated sugar, use a dry measure, scoop up the sugar, and level off the surface.

To measure brown sugar, pack it firmly into the cup measure with your fingers.

To measure baking powder, baking soda, and spices, dip exact-size measuring spoons into the container and level off the surface.

When measuring liquids, use a glass cup measure. Pour in the liquid, then bend over and check the amount at eye level.

Semisolid ingredients such as yogurt can be measured in either wet or dry cup measures. Most cooks find it easier to use the dry measure.

KEEPING PANCAKES AND WAFFLES WARM

If you're cooking for a crowd at breakfast, you may want to get a head start and cook some pancakes or waffles ahead.

Keep in mind that waffles are meant to be crisp, pancakes moist. Heat the oven to 200°F. or lower.

To keep pancakes warm and moist but not soggy, arrange them (as you complete a batch) slightly overlapping on a large platter. Cover loosely with foil and place on the oven rack.

To keep waffles warm or to reheat them, place them directly on the oven rack, or, for easier handling, on a wire cooling rack on the oven rack. Do not cover them. Freshly made waffles may be kept warm for at least 15 minutes without losing quality. Or let them cool, then reheat the same way.

FREEZING PANCAKES AND WAFFLES

Most pancakes and waffles freeze beautifully, and it's great to have a supply on hand. Freeze them with pieces of wax paper between so you can easily remove as many as you need. Store in an airtight container or zip-closure plastic bag (the type that state they are for freezer storage).

Reheat pancakes on a cookie sheet, waffles directly on the oven rack (or a cooling rack) for 5 to 6 minutes at 200°F. There is no need to defrost them first.

Waffles can also be successfully heated in a toaster. As for microwave heating, proceed with caution or leather will be your unpleasant reward. Wrap 1 to 3 pancakes or waffles in paper towels and heat on full power, in 10-second increments, until thawed and hot.

How Many Waffles?

You may have already noticed that most recipes give a batter yield. One reason is to let you vary the size of each pancake by using more or less batter.

But the main reason is so you can work out for yourself how many waffles each recipe will make in your particular waffle iron. One brand of waffle iron may take $\frac{1}{2}$ cup batter per batch, the next brand $\frac{3}{4}$ cup, and a third brand $1\frac{1}{4}$ cups. (Cooking times vary, too, and range from $1\frac{1}{2}$ minutes to 8 minutes, but that's easier to cope with.)

I suggest that you write on your particular waffle maker with a permanent marker the amount of batter to use for each batch. Of course not everyone has the extensive collection of waffle irons I acquired for testing, but it does save searching for the use-and-care booklet every time you want to make waffles. Also, figure out how many waffles you can make from the amount of batter in a particular recipe, and write that information next to the batter yield.

Making Perfect Pancakes

Even-colored, even-shaped pancakes come from having the batter at the right consistency, even heat, and the right heat for the particular batter, be it low, moderate, or higher.

Look for a griddle (electric is best) with plenty of cooking surface. Some griddles have a fat drainage moat (to catch bacon drippings, for example) that takes up a great deal of the space. A nonstick surface is helpful but not essential.

Alternatively, use a heavy skillet for pancakes. Again, choose one with plenty of bottom area (9 or 10 inches minimum) so you can cook several pancakes at a time.

Heat the griddle or skillet according to recipe directions. Unless a recipe specifies moderate or moderately low heat, test the griddle by flicking a couple of drops of water onto the surface. If they remain in one place and boil, the surface is not yet hot enough. If they vanish instantly, it is probably too hot. If the drops skitter across the surface (and then disappear), the griddle is ready for the first batch. Grease the griddle lightly by wiping a couple of drops of oil over the surface with a paper towel. Making pancakes is akin to dry baking—it is not frying. It might not be necessary to grease the griddle again, but if the pancakes stick wipe the oily paper towel across the surface again.

Many pancakes are a perfect size when made with 3 tablespoons of batter. You are not expected to measure three separate tablespoons of batter each time. Use a $\frac{1}{4}$-cup measure (4 tablespoons) and fill it three quarters full (3 tablespoons). Or use a ladle that holds 3 tablespoons.

Pour the batter onto the lightly greased surface, keeping the cup measure or ladle close to the surface and pouring into the center of the pool of batter for an even shape. The batter will spread a little, which will affect the number of pancakes you can cook at one time. After 2 or 3 minutes, carefully lift the edge of one pancake and look underneath. If the bottom looks a pleasing brown, slide a pancake turner under each one and gently turn them over. Let cook until brown on the second side. To keep pancakes warm or to freeze, see page 5.

Regard the first pancake of the day as a dry run. You're in charge. You may need to raise or lower the heat, depending on your range and the type of pan you are using. If the batter seems a little thick, stir in a tablespoon or two of milk or water. If it seems too thin (be sure to cook one or two first, some batters *are* thin), stir in a tablespoon or two more flour.

Making Perfect Waffles

When you eat a waffle, you're eating history. According to *Larousse Gastronomique,* waffles have been around at least since the end of the twelfth century. At that time they were cooked over direct heat between two hinged metal plates embossed with a decorative design. Those old-time waffles were as thin as wafers and probably more closely related to Italian pizzelle or Belgian gaufrette cookies than the thick waffles we love today. These waffles were an early street food because they were often sold outside churches on religious feast days.

If you're in the market for a waffle iron, an electric one with a nonstick finish is the way to go. Before you heat it, put it on a cookie sheet or heatproof tray on your countertop. The tray will protect the countertop and collect the inevitable crumbs and batter drips. Have handy a fairly stiff pastry brush for brushing out any crumbs between batches.

Keep the waffle maker closed while it heats. Before making the first waffle of the day brush the top and bottom grids lightly with vegetable oil or rub an oil-moistened piece of paper towel over them (without burning yourself). It is unlikely you will need to grease the grids again.

Pour the correct amount of batter onto the center of the waffle maker (if four-square or heart-shaped) or divide between the halves of a two-grid one. Usually you need to quickly spread the batter to the edges with a metal spatula.

Close the waffle maker. The waffle is ready when the iron will open easily. Some waffle makers have a light that goes out when the waffle is done. One or two emit a buzz, awful to the ears but handy if you tend to wander. Cooking time varies from brand to brand—the use-and-care booklet should shed light—but in all cases *waffles are ready when the waffle maker will open easily.* If you try and force it open you most likely will split the waffle in two (that's *your* breakfast). The cooked waffle should remain on the bottom grid. If it doesn't lift off easily, loosen the edges with a blunt tool (such as a table knife), taking care not to scrape or scratch a non-stick finish.

To keep waffles warm or to freeze, see page 5.

MAKING PERFECT CREPES

"Perfect" is perhaps not a good choice of word here because it rarely matters if a crepe is perfect since no one will see it unadorned. Crepes are well worth learning to make because they can be the foundation of a main dish, brunch dish, or dessert. They can be made well ahead of serving, and most can be frozen. Crepes are easy to make, but written instructions sound tedious. Once you get the hang of crepe making you will be able to cook up a pile in a relatively short time.

Cook the crepes in a skillet 6 ½ to 7 inches across the bottom, preferably with sloping sides. The skillet can have a nonstick finish or be made of cast iron or polished aluminum. There are numerous crepe pans in cookware stores. Follow any instructions for seasoning the pan before using it. (Nonstick finishes do not require seasoning.)

Crepe batter is much thinner than pancake or waffle batter, about the consistency of cream. Regard the first one or two crepes of the day as exploratory—while you get the heat just right and check the batter. If the batter seems too thick, stir in a tablespoon or two more water.

Many crepe recipes call for letting the batter stand for an hour before cooking. However, I did not find that it made any noticeable difference. But if it's more convenient, you can let the batter stand for an hour at room temperature or up to 24 hours in the refrigerator. Stir again before cooking.

Heat the skillet over moderately high heat. Either brush the surface with oil or moisten a corner of a paper towel with oil and wipe out the skillet. Crepes are not fried in oil. They are essentially "baked" on a dry surface (as are pancakes and waffles).

Many crepes use 3 tablespoons batter per crepe. Use a ¼-cup measure (4 tablespoons) and fill it three quarters full (3 tablespoons). Or find a ladle that holds just the right amount.

Dip the ladle or measure into the batter. Hold the skillet in your left hand (if right-handed) and pour the batter right in the center. At the same time, tilt the skillet in all directions so the batter flows over the bottom. When the bottom is covered, pour any excess batter back into the bowl. If there are big spaces, spoon in a tiny bit of extra batter. Put the skillet back on the heat and let the crepe cook a minute or two. (If you poured batter out of the skillet, cut off the "tail" left by the batter with the edge of a metal spatula.) The surface should begin to look matte (no longer liquid) and the edges should curl away from the skillet. Lift an edge of the crepe with the metal spatula and look underneath. If it seems a pleasing brown, slide the spatula underneath and turn the crepe over. Let cook a minute or so on the second side. The crepe will not brown evenly or thoroughly on the second side. Slide the crepe onto a cookie sheet or a piece of wax paper on the counter.

Each crepe should take only minutes to make. If it seems to be taking forever, increase the heat slightly.

To Serve with Pancakes and Waffles

Maple, sorghum, and cane syrups are three popular syrups. Honey makes a good syrup, though its natural flavor can dominate most pancakes and it is intensely sweet. (Try Honey Butter, page 127, instead.)

There is now a large variety of fruit syrups available, with quality and intensity of flavor varying among brands. Also try "pourable" fruit, fruit sweetened with juice concentrates.

Brown rice syrup and barley malt syrup, two alternative

sweeteners, are available in health food stores. Brown rice syrup has an earthy, almost bitter undertone that is not very complementary to pancakes. While barley malt syrup is a valuable baking ingredient, I found that as a topping its milder-than-molasses, stronger-than-honey taste easily overpowered delicate pancakes.

BREAKFAST

BEST-EVER PANCAKES
OR WAFFLES

MAKES 2 CUPS BATTER,
EIGHT 4-INCH PANCAKES,
ENOUGH FOR 4 PORTIONS

The whole wheat flour and the cinnamon give these a rich, full flavor. The recipe can easily be doubled and any extras frozen. Good with Brown Sugar Syrup, page 108, Santa Fe Spiced Syrup, page 109, Fresh Orange Syrup, page 110, or almost any syrup.

½ cup all-purpose flour
½ cup whole wheat flour
1 tablespoon granulated sugar
1 teaspoon baking powder
½ teaspoon baking soda
½ teaspoon ground cinnamon
¼ teaspoon salt
1 cup buttermilk, or ¾ cup plain yogurt plus ¼ cup water
1 large egg
2 tablespoons mild olive or vegetable oil
Oil for cooking

GRIDDLE OR LARGE SKILLET, OR WAFFLE IRON

Food processor method: Put the flours, sugar, baking powder, baking soda, cinnamon, and salt into a food processor. Process briefly to mix. Add the buttermilk, or yogurt and water, egg, and oil. Turn the machine on/off 3 or 4 times to make a smooth batter.

By hand: Put the flours, sugar, baking powder, baking soda, cinnamon, and salt into a large bowl. Stir to mix well.

Measure the buttermilk in a 2-cup glass measure. Add the egg and oil to the measuring cup. Beat with a fork or wire whisk to blend. Add to the flour mixture and stir to form a smooth batter.

Pancakes (see page 6): Heat the griddle or skillet over moderately high heat until it feels hot when you hold your hand directly above it. Lightly grease the griddle. For each pancake, pour $1/4$ cup batter onto the griddle. Cook 3 to 5 minutes, until bubbles appear on the surface and the undersides are golden brown. Adjust the heat if the pancakes are browning too fast. Turn the pancakes over and cook 1 to 2 minutes longer to brown the second side.

Waffles (see page 8): Heat the waffle iron; grease it lightly. Pour in the appropriate amount of batter and spread to the edges. Close and cook until the iron will open easily.

Keep warm in a 200°F. oven—pancakes on a plate and loosely covered to keep moist, waffles directly on the oven rack, uncovered, to stay crisp.

OLD-FASHIONED OAT PANCAKES OR WAFFLES

MAKES 3 CUPS BATTER,
TWENTY 2½-INCH PANCAKES,
ENOUGH FOR 6 TO 10 PORTIONS

Made with oats and no other grain at all, these are hearty and filling, perfect for a cold winter morning. Try them with Brown Sugar Syrup, page 108, or Honey Butter, page 127; almost any sweet topping suits them well. If you're making these with sour cream, use the real thing. Not all reduced-fat products work well here.

2 cups old-fashioned oats (not instant or quick)
1 tablespoon packed dark or light brown sugar
1½ teaspoons baking powder
½ teaspoon baking soda
½ teaspoon salt
1 cup sour cream or plain yogurt (reduce salt to ¼ teaspoon if using yogurt)
⅔ cup milk
2 large eggs
Oil for cooking

GRIDDLE OR LARGE SKILLET, OR WAFFLE IRON

Food processor method: Put the oats, sugar, baking powder, baking soda, and salt into a food processor. Process 1 to 2 minutes, until the oats are ground fine.

Add the sour cream or yogurt, milk, and eggs to the oat mixture. Turn the machine on/off 4 to 6 times, scraping the sides once, just until the batter is thoroughly mixed. Let the batter stand 5 minutes to thicken.

Pancakes (see page 6): Heat the griddle or skillet over moderately high heat until it feels hot when you hold your hand directly above it. Lightly grease the griddle. For each pancake, pour $\frac{1}{8}$ cup (2 tablespoons) batter onto the griddle. Cook 3 to 5 minutes, until the surface of the pancake looks dry (no bubbles will appear) and the undersides are golden brown. Adjust the heat if the pancakes are browning too fast. Turn the pancakes over and cook 1 to 2 minutes longer to brown the second side.

Waffles (see page 8): Heat the waffle iron (on medium if there's a choice). Grease the iron lightly. Pour in the appropriate amount of batter and spread to the edges. Close and cook until the iron will open easily.

Keep warm in a 200°F. oven—pancakes on a plate and loosely covered to keep moist, waffles directly on the oven rack, uncovered, to stay crisp.

SUPER-SIMPLE BAKED PANCAKE

MAKES 1 LARGE PANCAKE,
ENOUGH FOR 2 TO 4 PORTIONS

This could be the only pancake recipe you'll ever need because you can do so many things with it, even speedy versions of crepe recipes (see Light Meals, page 43, and Dessert, page 77). The batter can easily be doubled and baked in 2 skillets or pie pans side by side on the same oven rack. It's important that the oven be hot enough so the pancake develops high, crisp edges with a popoverlike middle. Serve with any syrup or fruit.

2 large eggs
½ cup milk
½ cup all-purpose flour
¼ teaspoon salt
Few grains of ground nutmeg
1 tablespoon mild olive or vegetable oil (olive oil tastes best here)

AN OVENPROOF SKILLET 9 TO 10 INCHES ACROSS THE BOTTOM, OR A 9-INCH GLASS OR METAL PIE PAN, OR AN 11 × 7-INCH BAKING DISH

Heat the oven to 450°F.

Food processor or blender method: Process the eggs, milk, flour, salt, and nutmeg to make a smooth batter.

By hand: Put the eggs and milk into a medium-size bowl. Beat with a wire whisk or electric mixer to blend well. Beat in the flour, salt, and nutmeg. If tiny lumps of flour remain visible, it's no problem.

Heat the oil in the skillet, pie pan, or baking dish in the oven for 5 minutes. When very hot, pour in the batter.

Bake uncovered 18 to 20 minutes without opening the oven door, until the pancake is puffed and crisp around the edges and golden brown in the middle. Cut in wedges to serve.

VARIATIONS

You can serve any of these with a knife and fork, but they also make great out-of-hand food. Cut the finished pancake in 4 or 6 wedges. Roll up each wedge from the pointed end and eat it like a tortilla.

CHILIES CON QUESO PANCAKE

While the Super-Simple Baked Pancake bakes, prepare 1 cup chopped fresh tomato, ⅓ cup thin-sliced scallions, 1 tablespoon minced jalapeño pepper, and 1 tablespoon chopped fresh cilantro. Toss together lightly in a bowl. Prepare ½ cup (2 ounces) shredded Monterey Jack or other melting cheese. Sprinkle the tomato mixture, then the cheese over the baked pancake. Bake about 3 minutes longer, until the cheese melts.

continued

Baked Egg and Cheese Pancake

While the Super-Simple Baked Pancake bakes, slightly beat 2 eggs with about ⅛ teaspoon salt and shred about ¼ cup (1 ounce) Jarlsberg, Gouda, Fontina, Gruyère, or other flavorful, firm cheese. Pour the eggs over the baked pancake, sprinkle with the cheese, and grind some pepper over the top. Bake about 1 minute longer, until the egg mixture is set.

Baked Lemon Pancake

Add ¼ teaspoon freshly grated lemon peel to the Super-Simple Baked Pancake batter and bake as directed. Sift (through strainer or dredger) about 1 tablespoon confectioners' sugar over the baked pancake. Sprinkle with 2 tablespoons freshly squeezed lemon juice and bake 2 minutes longer.

Margarita Pancake

Add ¼ teaspoon freshly grated lime peel to Super-Simple Baked Pancake batter and bake as directed. Sift about 2 teaspoons confectioners' sugar over the baked pancake. Sprinkle with 2 teaspoons freshly squeezed lime juice and ¼ teaspoon salt. Bake 2 minutes longer.

RICH BELGIAN-STYLE WAFFLES

MAKES 3 CUPS BATTER,
ENOUGH FOR 6 PORTIONS

Especially good with Brown Sugar Syrup, page 108, Hot Cranberry Kissel, page 113, or Strawberries and Cream Topping, page 117. You can make these in a regular waffle iron, or a Belgian-style one, which has deeper indentations.

1 large egg
1 cup regular or reduced-fat sour cream
½ cup milk
3 tablespoons mild olive oil or melted butter
¾ teaspoon baking powder
¼ teaspoon baking soda
¼ teaspoon salt
1 cup all-purpose flour
2 teaspoons granulated sugar
Oil for cooking

WAFFLE IRON, BELGIAN-STYLE FOR EXTRA-CRISP WAFFLES

Crack open the egg, letting the white fall into a deep narrow bowl. Put the yolk into a medium-size bowl. Add the sour cream, milk, oil or butter, baking powder, baking soda, salt, and flour to the yolk without mixing.

Beat the egg white with an electric mixer at high speed until soft peaks form when the beater is lifted. Add the sugar and beat until stiff peaks form.

continued

Transfer the beater to the other bowl and beat the ingredients at low speed until blended.

Using a rubber spatula, fold the beaten white into the flour mixture.

Heat the waffle iron (see page 8). Grease the iron lightly. Pour in the appropriate amount of batter and spread to the edges. Close and cook until the iron will open easily.

Keep the waffles warm in a 200°F. oven, directly on the oven rack, uncovered to stay crisp.

SOUR CREAM SILVER DOLLARS

MAKES 3¼ CUPS BATTER,
50 TO 55 SILVER DOLLAR–SIZED PANCAKES,
ENOUGH FOR 10 TO 12 PORTIONS

Delicious with Maple-Apple Topping, page 124, Fresh Applesauce, page 123, or any syrup (I like Santa Fe Spiced Syrup, page 109).

⅓ cup all-purpose flour
3 tablespoons granulated sugar
1 teaspoon baking soda
¼ teaspoon salt
2 cups regular or reduced-fat sour cream
4 large eggs
1 teaspoon vanilla extract
Oil for cooking

GRIDDLE OR LARGE SKILLET

Food processor method: Put the flour, sugar, baking soda, and salt into a food processor. Process a few seconds to mix. Add the sour cream, eggs, and vanilla. Turn the machine on/off 5 or 6 times, scraping the sides of the bowl once, to make a smooth, creamy batter.

By hand: Mix the flour, sugar, baking soda, and salt in a medium-size bowl. Add the sour cream, eggs, and vanilla. Beat with a wire whisk or wooden spoon just until the dry ingredients are moistened.

continued

Heat the griddle or skillet over low heat until it feels warm when you hold your hand directly above it. Lightly grease the griddle. For each pancake, drop 1 tablespoon batter onto the griddle. Cook 30 seconds to 2 minutes, until bubbles appear all over the surface and start to break and the undersides are golden brown. Adjust the heat if the pancakes are browning too fast. Turn the pancakes over and cook 1 to $1\frac{1}{2}$ minutes longer to brown the second side. (These pancakes are thin and delicate; it takes a quick movement with a thin metal spatula to turn them without breaking them.)

Keep the pancakes warm in a 200°F. oven on a plate, loosely covered to keep them moist.

SOURDOUGH PANCAKES
OR WAFFLES

MAKES 4 CUPS BATTER,
32 THIN 3½- TO 4-INCH PANCAKES,
ENOUGH FOR 6 TO 8 PORTIONS

With their yeasty aroma and sourdough flavor these are delicious with any syrup or topping. The batter makes especially crisp and light waffles. Both pancakes and waffles freeze well. Start the batter at least 14 hours before cooking.

1¾ cups milk
¼ cup warm water
2 tablespoons granulated sugar
1 envelope active dry yeast
3 large eggs
¼ cup mild olive or vegetable oil
1 teaspoon salt
2 cups all-purpose flour
Oil for cooking

GRIDDLE OR LARGE SKILLET, OR WAFFLE IRON

Heat the milk until very hot in a microwave-safe container for 2 minutes on high, or in a small saucepan over moderate heat until bubbles appear around the edge. Remove from the heat.

Mix the water, sugar, and yeast in a large bowl or 2-quart glass measure. Let stand 5 minutes. Yeast granules should swell and look creamy. (If yeast doesn't change, it may no longer be active, in which case choose another recipe or get fresh yeast.)

Add the eggs, oil, and salt to the yeast mixture. Beat with a wire whisk or wooden spoon to blend well. Whisk in the hot milk, then the flour, to make a creamy batter. Cover and let stand 1½ hours at room temperature.

Stir or whisk batter (which should be bubbly on the surface). Cover and refrigerate at least 12 hours and up to 48 hours. Stir batter before cooking.

Pancakes (see page 6): Heat the griddle or skillet over moderately high heat until it feels hot when you hold your hand directly above it. Lightly grease the griddle. For each pancake, pour ⅛ cup (2 tablespoons) batter onto the griddle. Cook 1 to 2 minutes, until lots of bubbles appear on the surface and start to burst and the undersides are golden brown. Adjust the heat if the pancakes are browning too fast. Turn the pancakes over and cook 1 to 2 minutes longer to brown the second side.

Waffles (see page 8): Heat the waffle iron; grease it lightly. Pour in the appropriate amount of batter and spread to the edges. Close and cook until the iron will open easily.

Keep warm in a 200°F. oven—pancakes on a plate and loosely covered to keep moist, waffles directly on the oven rack, uncovered, to stay crisp.

BUCKWHEAT PANCAKES
OR WAFFLES

MAKES ALMOST 2½ CUPS BATTER,
TEN 4-INCH PANCAKES,
ENOUGH FOR 5 PORTIONS

Serve with maple or fruit syrup, or with tart preserves, such as lingonberry.

⅔ cup all-purpose flour
⅓ cup buckwheat flour
1 tablespoon granulated sugar
1 teaspoon baking powder
½ teaspoon baking soda
¼ teaspoon salt
1 cup plain yogurt
¼ cup water
1 large egg
2 tablespoons mild olive or vegetable oil
Oil for cooking

GRIDDLE OR LARGE SKILLET, OR WAFFLE IRON

Food processor method: Put the flours, sugar, baking powder, baking soda, and salt into a food processor. Process briefly to mix.

Add the yogurt, water, egg, and oil to the flour mixture. Process 10 to 15 seconds, scraping the sides once, just until well mixed.

continued

By hand: Put the flours, sugar, baking powder, baking soda, and salt into a large bowl. Stir to mix well. Measure the yogurt and water in a 2-cup glass measure. Add the egg and oil to the measuring cup. Beat with a fork or wire whisk to blend well. Add to the flour mixture and stir until well blended.

Pancakes (see page 6): Heat the griddle or skillet over moderate heat until it feels hot when you hold your hand directly above it. Lightly grease the griddle. For each pancake, pour $1/4$ cup batter onto the griddle. Cook 2 to 3 minutes, until bubbles appear on the surface and the undersides are golden brown. Adjust the heat if the pancakes are browning too fast. Turn the pancakes over and cook 1 to 2 minutes longer to brown the second side.

Waffles (see page 8): Heat the waffle iron; grease it lightly. Pour in the appropriate amount of batter and spread to the edges. Close and cook until the iron will open easily.

Keep warm in a 200°F. oven—pancakes on a plate and loosely covered to keep moist, waffles directly on the oven rack, uncovered, to stay crisp.

TOASTED HAZELNUT WAFFLES

MAKES 2½ CUPS BATTER,
ENOUGH FOR 3 OR 4 PORTIONS

I love hazelnuts, so naturally these are one of my favorite waffles. I like them with Brown Sugar Syrup, page 108, or maple syrup. They make a spectacular dessert, too, with a scoop of praline ice cream or with a little Praline Filling, page 87.

¾ cup untoasted hazelnuts (about 4 ounces)
1 cup all-purpose flour
2 tablespoons granulated sugar
1 teaspoon baking powder
½ teaspoon baking soda
¼ teaspoon salt
1 cup buttermilk or plain yogurt
1 large egg
3 tablespoons mild olive or vegetable oil
Oil for cooking

WAFFLE IRON

Heat the oven to 350°F. Spread the hazelnuts in a baking pan and bake 8 to 10 minutes, shaking the pan once or twice, until the nuts smell toasty and turn light brown.

Wrap the nuts in a dish towel and rub to loosen the skins. Pick out the nuts; some skins will adhere and it's fine to use those nuts.

Chop the nuts fairly fine in a food processor. Add the flour, sugar, baking powder, baking soda, and salt to the nuts. Process to blend well. Add the buttermilk or yogurt, egg, and oil; process a few seconds to blend, scraping down the sides once.

Heat the waffle iron (see page 8) on medium (if there's a choice). Grease the iron lightly. Pour in the appropriate amount of batter and spread to the edges. Close and cook until the iron will open easily.

Keep the waffles warm in a 200°F. oven directly on the oven rack, uncovered, to stay crisp.

THREE-GRAIN PANCAKES
OR WAFFLES

Good with any syrup.

⅔ cup whole wheat flour
⅓ cup barley flour
⅓ cup millet flour (see Note)
2 tablespoons packed light brown sugar
1½ teaspoons baking powder
½ teaspoon baking soda
¼ teaspoon salt
1½ cups buttermilk or plain yogurt
2 large eggs
¼ cup mild olive or vegetable oil
Oil for cooking

GRIDDLE OR LARGE SKILLET, OR WAFFLE IRON

Food processor method: Put the flours, sugar, baking powder, baking soda, and salt into a food processor. Process briefly to mix.

Add the buttermilk or yogurt, eggs, and oil to the flour mixture. Process 10 to 15 seconds, scraping the sides once, just until well mixed.

continued

By hand: Put the flours, baking powder, baking soda, and salt into a large bowl. Stir to mix well.

Measure the buttermilk or yogurt in a 1-quart glass measure. Add the oil, sugar, and eggs to the measuring cup. Beat with a fork or wire whisk to blend well. Pour over the flour mixture and stir until well blended.

Pancakes (see page 6): Heat the griddle or skillet over moderate heat until it feels hot when you hold your hand directly above it. Lightly grease the griddle. For each pancake, pour a scant ¼ cup batter onto the griddle. Cook 3 to 4 minutes, until the edges look cooked and the undersides are golden brown. Adjust the heat if the pancakes are browning too fast. Turn the pancakes over and cook 1 to 2 minutes longer to brown the second side.

Waffles (see page 8): Heat the waffle iron; grease it lightly. Pour in the appropriate amount of batter and spread to the edges. Close and cook until the iron will open easily.

Keep warm in a 200°F. oven—pancakes on a plate and loosely covered to keep moist, waffles directly on the oven rack, uncovered, to stay crisp.

NOTE: If you can only buy whole millet or millet meal, grind ⅓ cup as fine as possible in an electric blender (a food processor does not work for this).

VARIATIONS

WHEAT, CORNMEAL, AND BROWN RICE PANCAKES OR WAFFLES
Makes 3½ cups batter, enough for sixteen 3½-inch pancakes

Use 1 cup all-purpose flour, 1 cup brown rice flour, and
⅓ cup cornmeal for the flours specified.

WHOLE WHEAT, BARLEY, AND CORNMEAL PANCAKES OR WAFFLES
Mapkes 3 cups batter, enough for twelve 4-inch pancakes

Use ⅔ cup whole wheat flour, ⅓ cup barley flour, and
⅓ cup cornmeal for the flours specified.

CHEESE PANCAKES OR WAFFLES

Delicious with Canadian bacon for breakfast, or with hot red pepper jelly or salsa for supper.

1 cup all-purpose flour
1 teaspoon baking powder
½ teaspoon baking soda
¼ teaspoon salt
⅛ teaspoon freshly ground black pepper
⅛ teaspoon ground red pepper (cayenne) or crushed red pepper
  flakes
1¼ cups buttermilk, or 1½ cups plain yogurt
1 large egg
2 tablespoons mild olive or vegetable oil
4 ounces Gouda cheese, shredded (about 1 cup)
Oil for cooking

GRIDDLE OR LARGE SKILLET, OR WAFFLE IRON

Food processor method: Put the flour, baking powder, baking soda, salt, and black and red peppers into a food processor. Process briefly to blend.

Add the buttermilk or yogurt, egg, and oil to the flour mixture. Process briefly to mix. Scrape down the sides. Add the cheese and turn the machine on/off 2 or 3 times just to mix the cheese in.

By hand: Put the flour, baking powder, baking soda, salt, and peppers into a medium-size bowl. Stir to mix well.

Measure the buttermilk or yogurt in a 2-cup glass measure. Add the egg and oil to the measuring cup. Beat with a fork or wire whisk to blend well. Pour into the flour mixture and stir just until well mixed. Stir in the cheese.

Pancakes (see page 6): Heat the griddle or skillet over moderate heat until it feels hot when you hold your hand directly above it. Lightly grease the griddle. For each pancake, pour 3 tablespoons batter (a $1/4$-cup measure three quarters full) onto the griddle. Spread out the batter slightly. Cook 2 to 4 minutes, until bubbles appear on the surface and the undersides are golden brown. Adjust the heat if the pancakes are browning too fast. Turn the pancakes over and cook about 2 minutes longer to brown the second side.

Waffles (see page 8): Heat the waffle iron; grease it lightly. Pour in the appropriate amount of batter and spread to the edges. Close and cook until the iron will open easily.

Keep warm in a 200°F. oven—pancakes on a plate and loosely covered to keep moist, waffles directly on the oven rack, uncovered, to stay crisp.

BROWN RICE PANCAKES

MAKES 2 CUPS BATTER,
ABOUT TWELVE 3-INCH PANCAKES,
ENOUGH FOR 3 OR 4 PORTIONS

Friends on a gluten-free diet will especially appreciate these. Besides being wheat-free they are also very low in fat. A version that's also milk-free follows.

2 large eggs
1/3 cup plain yogurt
1/4 cup milk
1/2 cup brown rice flour
1/4 cup granulated sugar
1/2 teaspoon baking soda
1/4 teaspoon salt
Oil for cooking

GRIDDLE OR LARGE SKILLET

Crack open the eggs, letting the whites fall into a deep, narrow bowl; put the yolks into a medium-size bowl.

Add the yogurt and milk to the yolks. Stir to mix well. Stir in the brown rice flour, 2 tablespoons of the sugar, the baking soda, and salt.

Beat the egg whites with an electric mixer at high speed until soft peaks form when the beater is lifted. Add the remaining 2 tablespoons sugar and beat until stiff peaks form.

Reduce the mixer speed to low. Add about half the yolk mixture. Beat a few seconds, just until the mixtures begin to combine, then add the remaining yolk mixture and beat (at the lowest speed) only until the mixture is just blended.

To make the pancakes (see page 6): Heat the griddle or skillet over moderately low heat until it feels warm when you hold your hand directly above it. Lightly grease the griddle. For each pancake, pour 3 tablespoons batter (a ¼-cup measure three quarters full) onto the griddle. Cook 3 to 5 minutes, until bubbles appear on the surface and the undersides are golden brown. Turn the pancakes over and cook 1 to 2 minutes longer to brown the second side.

Keep the pancakes warm in a 200°F. oven—on a plate, loosely covered to keep them moist.

VARIATION

MILK-FREE, WHEAT-FREE PANCAKES

Omit milk and yogurt from the recipe. Puree in a blender or food processor ⅓ cup soft tofu, 2 tablespoons water, 2 tablespoons sugar, and the egg yolks. When smooth, add the brown rice flour, baking soda, and salt. Puree until blended. Add to the beaten whites and continue as directed above.

MAINE BLUEBERRY
BUTTERMILK PANCAKES

MAKES 2½ CUPS BATTER,
ABOUT FOURTEEN 3-INCH PANCAKES,
ENOUGH FOR 4 OR 5 PORTIONS

Very small blueberries—sometimes called "wild" blueberries—work best in these mild, soothing pancakes. Good with a fruit topping such as Blueberry Sauce, page 112, or with store-bought "pourable" fruit. A wow with Raspberry Syrup, page 115.

1½ cups fresh or frozen blueberries

SUGAR AND SPICE TOPPING
⅓ cup granulated sugar
½ teaspoon ground cinnamon
¼ teaspoon ground or freshly grated nutmeg

PANCAKES
1 cup all-purpose flour
2 tablespoons granulated sugar
1 teaspoon baking powder
½ teaspoon baking soda
¼ teaspoon salt
¼ teaspoon ground or freshly grated nutmeg
1 cup buttermilk, or 1 cup plain yogurt plus 3 tablespoons
*   water*

1 large egg
2 tablespoons unsalted butter, melted
Oil for cooking

GRIDDLE OR LARGE SKILLET

Rinse fresh blueberries, removing any stems or green berries. Pat dry with paper towels. Do not rinse or thaw frozen berries. Mix the Sugar and Spice Topping ingredients.

Put the flour, sugar, baking powder, baking soda, salt, and nutmeg into a large bowl. Stir to mix well.

Measure the buttermilk or yogurt and water in a 2-cup glass measure. Add the egg and butter to the measuring cup. Beat with a fork or wire whisk to blend well. Add to the flour mixture and stir gently until well blended. Stir in the blueberries.

To make pancakes (see page 6): Heat the griddle or skillet over moderate heat until it feels hot when you hold your hand directly above it. Lightly grease the griddle. For each pancake, pour 3 tablespoons batter (a ¼-cup measure three quarters full) onto the griddle. Cook 3 to 5 minutes, until bubbles appear on the surface and the undersides are golden brown. Adjust the heat if the pancakes are browning too fast. Turn the pancakes over and cook 1 to 2 minutes longer to brown the second side.

Keep the pancakes warm in a 200°F. oven on a plate, loosely covered to keep them moist. Sprinkle with Sugar and Spice Topping before serving.

BREAD AND CHEESE PANCAKE

MAKES 1 LARGE PANCAKE,
ENOUGH FOR
1 OR 2 PORTIONS

This makes a delicious breakfast or a light meal and is a great way to use up stale bread. For the lightest pancake let the mixture soak at least 1 hour. I usually make the batter in the evening (while I'm in the kitchen getting dinner) and cook it one or two mornings later.

2 cups cubed white or whole wheat bread (remove crusts)
2 large eggs
½ cup milk
1 ounce Cheddar or Gouda cheese, diced (¼ cup)
1 tablespoon freshly grated Parmesan cheese, or a generous
*   pinch of salt*
2 teaspoons butter

A NONSTICK SKILLET, 6 INCHES ACROSS THE BOTTOM

Put the bread, eggs, and milk into a food processor. Add the cheeses. Process a few seconds until well blended.

If you wish, pour into a bowl, cover, and refrigerate.

To cook, melt the butter in the skillet over moderately high heat and spread the butter over the bottom of the pan. Pour in the bread mixture. Cover the pan, reduce the heat to low, and cook until the mixture is no longer liquid in the center, 8 to 10 minutes.

Remove from the heat. Let stand, covered, 1 to 2 minutes. Loosen the pancake around the edges. Turn the skillet upside down over a plate.

LIGHT MEALS

FRESH CORN AND
CHEESE PANCAKE

I make this at least once a week in the corn season, especially when white corn is in the market. If I have ham on hand I sometimes sprinkle about 2 tablespoons chopped ham on top of the batter about halfway through cooking.

*1½ cups kernels cut from 1 large ear fresh corn or frozen corn
    kernels*
1 ounce sharp Cheddar cheese
2 large eggs
¼ cup milk
½ teaspoon salt
¼ teaspoon freshly ground pepper
2 teaspoons butter

A NONSTICK SKILLET, 6 TO 7 INCHES ACROSS THE BOTTOM

To cut fresh corn off the cob, hold the corn upright on a plate and slice the kernels off from about midway to the bottom. Then hold the cut part while you slice off the remaining kernels.

Cut the cheese into pieces about the size of green peas; 1 ounce is a rounded ¼ cup.

Put the corn and cheese into a food processor. Process a

few seconds to chop. Add the eggs, milk, salt, and pepper. Process until the batter is fairly smooth.

Melt the butter in the skillet over moderately high heat. Spread the butter over the bottom of the pan. Pour in the corn mixture. Reduce the heat to low. Cover the pan tightly with a lid or with foil and cook 10 to 15 minutes, or until the corn mixture looks a more intense yellow and is no longer liquid in the center.

Loosen the pancake around the edges and shake the pan to make sure it is not sticking. Turn the pancake upside down onto a plate and serve whole or cut into wedges.

NOTE: For 4 to 6 portions, double the recipe and cook in a nonstick skillet 8 $\frac{1}{2}$ to 9 inches across the bottom. The cooking time is about the same.

PETER ROSE'S DUTCH CHEESE PANCAKE

MAKES 1 LARGE PANCAKE, ENOUGH FOR 2 OR 3 PORTIONS

There are little pops of melted cheese throughout this hearty pancake, which is ready in short order. With a crunchy salad it makes a comforting supper. Food historian Peter Rose says the custom of making a pancake for a meal goes back at least to the sixteenth century. (Old manuscripts and paintings provide evidence.) Holland was (and still is) a very dairy country, so milk was easily available. Making a pancake such as this required only the simplest of ingredients and tools, and a very small amount of fuel.

3 to 4 ounces Gouda cheese
1 cup milk
1 large egg
1 cup all-purpose flour
½ teaspoon curry powder
⅛ teaspoon ground or freshly grated nutmeg
1 tablespoon butter

A NONSTICK OR HEAVY SKILLET, 9 INCHES ACROSS THE BOTTOM

Cut the cheese into pieces about the size of green peas; 3 ounces is about ¾ cup.

Put the remaining ingredients, except the butter, into a food processor or blender in the order given. Process to make a smooth batter, stopping the machine and scraping down the sides once or twice.

If using a food processor, sprinkle the cheese over the surface of the batter and turn the machine on/off once. If using a blender, sprinkle the cheese over the surface and stir in with a rubber spatula.

Heat the skillet over moderate heat. Add the butter and when melted, spread over the bottom of the pan. Pour in the batter. Reduce the heat to moderately low and cook 5 to 6 minutes, until firm and brown on the bottom and most of the batter on top has thickened but not yet completely set. Loosen the pancake with a pancake turner or by shaking the pan back and forth several times.

Slide the pancake cooked side down onto a flat plate. Put the skillet over the pancake, and turn the skillet and plate over together (the pancake will be back in the skillet). Cook until browned and set on the bottom, 3 to 4 minutes longer.

Slide the pancake onto a serving plate, cut into wedges, and serve.

CRISP NOODLE PANCAKE WITH STIR-FRIED CHICKEN

MAKES 1 PANCAKE, ENOUGH FOR 2 PORTIONS

T his looks appealing and tastes great but it's definitely for a casual dinner *à deux* since it's impossible to eat neatly! The pancake—essentially it's just compressed pasta—uses only three ingredients and is good with lots of other foods. It's a great reason to always cook a little extra spaghetti. Start the pancake and while it is cooking get all the ingredients ready for the stir-fry. The actual stir-frying takes no more than 5 minutes.

2 cups cold cooked thin spaghetti or linguine (4 ounces before cooking)
1 teaspoon dark sesame oil (optional, but good)
1 tablespoon vegetable oil

A NONSTICK SKILLET WITH SLOPING SIDES, 6 TO 7 INCHES ACROSS THE BOTTOM

Heat the oven to 200° F. Toss the spaghetti or linguine with the sesame oil to coat.

Heat the vegetable oil in the skillet over moderate heat. Add the spaghetti or linguine, spread evenly in pan, and press down firmly with a pancake turner. Place a sheet of foil over the noodles and set a plate (small enough to fit inside the skillet but large enough to cover the noodles) on top of the foil. Place two 1-pound cans on the plate to compress the noodles. Cook 8 to 10 minutes, until the noodles are browned on the bottom. Uncover the pancake. Carefully slide it out onto a flat plate, then flip it over back into the pan. Cook until the second side is browned, about 5 minutes. Slide the pancake onto a heatproof serving platter, cover loosely with foil, and keep warm in the oven. Just before serving, cut the pancake into wedges and spoon the Stir-Fried Chicken over it.

STIR-FRIED CHICKEN

8 ounces boneless, skinless chicken breast
4 or 5 scallions
1 small red bell pepper
⅓ cup chicken broth
1 tablespoon soy sauce
1 teaspoon cornstarch
1½ tablespoons vegetable oil
1 teaspoon minced fresh garlic
1 teaspoon minced or grated fresh gingerroot

Cut the chicken crosswise in ¼-inch strips. Trim the scallions and cut in 1-inch lengths, enough to make 1 cup. Slice enough red pepper into ¼-inch strips to make 1 cup. Mix the chicken broth, soy sauce, and cornstarch in a small bowl.

Shortly before serving, heat 1 tablespoon oil (use the same skillet you used for the pancake) over moderately high heat. Add the garlic and ginger and stir-fry for 30 seconds. Add the chicken and cook 2 to 3 minutes, stirring and tossing almost constantly, until the chicken turns white. Remove the chicken to a plate, cover loosely, and keep warm in the oven with the pancake. Add the remaining $1/2$ tablespoon oil to the skillet. Add the scallions and red pepper and stir-fry for 2 minutes. Stir the soy sauce mixture and stir into the vegetables in the skillet. The sauce will thicken and boil very quickly.

Add the chicken and any juices that have collected on the plate and toss to mix. Spoon over the noodle pancake and serve.

CORNMEAL WAFFLES WITH QUICK CHILI AND SOUR CREAM

MAKES 2¼ CUPS BATTER AND 3 CUPS CHILI, ENOUGH FOR 4 PORTIONS

Make the waffle batter first so it stands a few minutes and thickens while you start the Quick Chili (recipe below). Then, while the chili simmers, make the waffles. Both can also be made ahead and reheated. Spoon the chili over the waffles and serve with sour cream and sliced scallions for an excellent meal.

½ cup cornmeal
½ cup all-purpose flour
1 tablespoon granulated sugar
1 teaspoon baking powder
½ teaspoon baking soda
½ teaspoon salt
1 cup buttermilk, or ¾ cup plain yogurt plus ¼ cup water
1 large egg
3 tablespoons mild olive or vegetable oil
Oil for cooking

WAFFLE IRON

Put the cornmeal, flour, sugar, baking powder, baking soda, and salt into a food processor (or a large bowl). Process briefly (or stir) to mix.

Add the buttermilk or yogurt and water, egg, and oil to

cornmeal mixture. Process a few seconds (or stir with a wooden spoon), scraping the sides once, just until blended.

Heat the waffle iron (see page 8). Grease the iron lightly. Pour in the appropriate amount of batter and spread to the edges. Close and cook until the iron will open easily.

Keep the waffles warm in a 200°F. oven, directly on the oven rack, uncovered, to stay crisp.

QUICK CHILI

½ pound lean ground beef
One 16-ounce jar hot or medium thick-and-chunky salsa
One 15-ounce can pinto beans, rinsed and drained

Brown the meat in a medium-size skillet over moderately high heat for about 5 minutes, stirring to break up chunks. Drain off any fat.

Add the salsa and beans to the meat. Bring to a simmer. Reduce the heat to low, cover, and cook 25 to 30 minutes, stirring 3 or 4 times, until the flavors are blended.

POLENTA PANCAKE WITH GREENS AND HAM

Perfect comfort food for lovers of greens and polenta. *Polenta* is the Italian word for good old Southern cornmeal mush.

2 cups water
⅔ cup yellow cornmeal (regular, not coarse-ground)
½ cup freshly grated Parmesan cheese (2 ounces)
1 tablespoon unsalted butter
½ teaspoon salt
⅛ teaspoon freshly ground pepper
2 large eggs
1 tablespoon olive oil

GREENS AND HAM

Enough greens (such as turnip, collard, mustard, or beet greens, kale, Swiss chard, chicory, escarole, or broccoli rabe, alone or any combination of 3) to make about 7 firmly packed cups
4 ounces flavorful ham in 1 thick slice (can be Smithfield, baked Virginia, or other)
1 tablespoon olive oil, preferably extra virgin
1 teaspoon minced fresh garlic
Salt and freshly ground pepper

continued

A NONSTICK SKILLET WITH SLOPING SIDES, ABOUT 10 INCHES ACROSS THE BOTTOM

Bring the water to a boil in a heavy, 2- to 3-quart saucepan. Over moderate heat, whisk or stir the water constantly while slowly sprinkling in the cornmeal. Reduce the heat to low and cook about 3 minutes, until thick and smooth, stirring constantly (the spoon will leave a trail so you can see the bottom of the pan).

Remove the pan from the heat. Stir in the cheese, butter, salt, and pepper. Let cool 5 minutes. Stir in the eggs one at a time.

Heat the oven to 200°F. to keep the pancake warm. Heat the oil in the skillet over moderately high heat. Spread the cornmeal mixture evenly in the skillet. Reduce the heat to moderate and cook 10 to 15 minutes, until golden brown on the bottom and the surface no longer looks very wet.

Meanwhile, pull the turnip, collard, mustard greens, or kale leaves off the coarse stems, or trim the coarse bottom half of broccoli rabe stems. If using Swiss chard or beet greens, use both the stems and leaves. Measure 7 firmly packed cups of greens (a little more or less is fine).

Scrunch up handfuls of the greens on a cutting board and cut them across in about 1/2-inch widths.

Wash the greens in 2 or 3 changes of cold water, or until they are no longer gritty, and drain them in a colander.

Cut the ham in 1/4-inch pieces (you'll have about 3/4 cup).

Over moderately high heat, heat the oil in a large saucepan (one about 12 inches wide will give you plenty of room to stir the greens).

Add the greens, garlic, and ham to the pan. Cook uncovered 5 to 7 minutes, until the greens wilt, tossing the greens often with 2 wooden spoons so they heat evenly. The greens will cook down to about 1½ cups. Season with salt and pepper to taste. If you prefer the greens more cooked, you may cover the pan and cook them about 5 minutes longer.

Loosen the polenta pancake with a plastic spatula. Shake the skillet gently to make sure the pancake is free from the bottom. Carefully slide the pancake (cooked side down) out onto a flat plate or a pizza pan. Put the skillet over the pancake and turn the skillet and plate over together (the pancake will be back in the skillet). Cook the pancake about 8 minutes longer, shaking the pan occasionally to loosen it.

When the pancake is golden brown on the bottom, slide it onto a warm serving platter (or you can serve it from the skillet). Keep warm uncovered in the oven until serving time. Cut into wedges and serve with greens alongside.

KOREAN SCALLION PANCAKES
WITH BEAN SPROUT SALAD

MAKES 1 CUP BATTER,
TWO 8- TO 9-INCH PANCAKES,
AND 1½ CUPS SALAD,
ENOUGH FOR 2 PORTIONS

Make the salad first so the flavors have time to blend. A nice way to eat this is to spoon the salad on top of the pancakes, roll the pancakes up, and eat them out of hand.

⅓ cup all-purpose flour
2 large eggs
2 tablespoons water
1 tablespoon plus 2 teaspoons mild olive or vegetable oil
½ teaspoon salt
5 scallions
1 small hot fresh chili or pickled jalapeño pepper
Bean Sprout Salad (recipe follows)

A GRIDDLE OR NONSTICK SKILLET, 8 TO 9 INCHES ACROSS THE BOTTOM

Put the flour, eggs, water, 1 tablespoon oil, and salt into a medium-size bowl. Beat with a wire whisk or electric mixer to make a smooth, very thick batter.

Trim the scallions, leaving the white part with about 3 inches of the green tops. Cut the scallions in half lengthwise, then slice thinly crosswise. Add to the batter.

Cut the chili in half; remove the seeds and core. Mince the chili as finely as possible and stir into the batter.

Heat 1 teaspoon of the remaining oil in the griddle or skillet over moderately high heat. When the griddle is very hot, pour in half the batter (about ½ cup). With a metal spatula, spread it to an 8-inch pancake about ⅛ inch thick.

When the bottom is lightly browned, about 1 minute, flip the pancake over and cook 1 to 2 minutes longer.

Lift the pancake to a warmed plate. Make a second pancake with the remaining oil and batter. Serve right away with the salad.

BEAN SPROUT SALAD

1 tablespoon sesame seeds
1½ cups mung bean sprouts (4 ounces)
2 tablespoons rice wine vinegar or cider vinegar
2 tablespoons soy sauce
1 teaspoon granulated sugar
1 teaspoon dark sesame oil (optional)
½ teaspoon minced fresh garlic

Toast the sesame seeds in a small heavy skillet or saucepan over moderate heat for 4 to 5 minutes, tossing frequently, until golden brown.

Put the toasted seeds into a medium-size bowl. Add the remaining ingredients and toss to mix. Let stand at room temperature about 30 minutes (but not more than 1 hour) for the flavor to develop.

VERMONT BAKED CHEDDAR AND APPLE PANCAKE

MAKES 1 LARGE PANCAKE, ENOUGH FOR 2 OR 3 PORTIONS

The time-honored combination of apple and cheese (as in a snack or a pie) is presented here in a traditional Vermont pancake. It can be enjoyed as a comforting breakfast or Sunday supper. Serve with a little maple syrup to bring out the flavor.

⅓ cup all-purpose flour
2 tablespoons whole wheat flour or additional all-purpose flour
2 tablespoons granulated sugar
⅔ cup milk
2 large eggs
Few grains of salt
¾ cup (about 3 ounces) shredded sharp Cheddar cheese
1 small or ½ large Granny Smith or other tart apple
1 tablespoon unsalted butter
Confectioners' sugar

AN OVENPROOF SKILLET, 10 TO 12 INCHES ACROSS THE BOTTOM

Check to make sure one rack is in the center of the oven and heat the oven to 375°F.

Put the flour(s), 1 tablespoon sugar, milk, eggs, and salt into a food processor, blender, or medium-size bowl. Process (or whisk) to make a smooth batter. Stir the cheese into the bowl, or add to the food processor or blender and turn the machine on/off once or twice to mix.

Peel, quarter, and core the apple. Cut into thin wedges.

Melt the butter in the skillet over moderately high heat. Add the apple and cook for 2 to 3 minutes, until the apple is tender and just beginning to brown. Sprinkle the remaining 1 tablespoon sugar over the apple as it cooks. Remove from the heat.

Spread the apple evenly over the bottom of the pan. Pour the batter over the apple.

Bake uncovered about 30 minutes, or until the pancake is browned and very puffy. Remove from the oven (the pancake will quickly collapse). Sprinkle thickly with confectioners' sugar (sifted through a strainer or dredger) and cut in wedges to serve.

BLACK BEAN–STUFFED CREPES WITH FRESH TOMATO SALSA AND SOUR CREAM

MAKES 2 CUPS BATTER
AND 2 CUPS BEAN FILLING,
ABOUT 10 FILLED CREPES,
ENOUGH FOR 4 OR 5 PORTIONS

Wonderful anytime with sour cream and Fresh Tomato Salsa, page 126. The filled crepes freeze well, but for a revisionist version you can be eating 30 minutes from now, see the variation at the end of the recipe.

CREPES

1 cup milk
2 large eggs
3 tablespoons mild olive or vegetable oil
½ teaspoon salt
¾ cup all-purpose flour
Oil for cooking

BEAN FILLING

2 teaspoons mild olive or vegetable oil
½ cup chopped onion
1 teaspoon ground cumin seeds
One 15- to 16-ounce can black beans, undrained

¼ teaspoon salt
¼ teaspoon freshly ground pepper
2 tablespoons chopped fresh cilantro leaves
2 tablespoons regular or reduced-fat sour cream, plus additional for serving

A CREPE PAN OR NONSTICK SKILLET, 6 ½ TO 7 INCHES ACROSS THE BOTTOM

To make the crepes: Put the milk, eggs, oil, salt, and flour into a food processor or blender in the order given. Process to make a smooth, thin batter, scraping down the sides once or twice.

Follow the directions for making crepes on page 9, using about 3 tablespoons batter for each. Crepes may be made ahead and refrigerated or frozen before or after filling.

To make the filling: Heat the oil in a small skillet over moderate heat. Stir in the onion and cumin. Cook 3 to 5 minutes, until the onion is translucent. Stir in the beans and their liquid, salt, and pepper. Cover and cook over low heat for 5 to 6 minutes, stirring once or twice, for the flavors to blend. Add a little water if the mixture gets dry. Remove from the heat. Stir in the cilantro and sour cream.

To assemble: Spread 3 or 4 crepes at a time out on a work surface, with the first-cooked (brownest) side down. Put a generous tablespoonful of the filling on each, slightly off center. Fold the crepe over to make a half circle, then fold over again to make a triangle. (Filled crepes may be covered and refrigerated for up to 3 days or brushed lightly with melted butter and frozen for up to 3 months.)

To serve: Heat a griddle or large skillet over moderate heat. Brush lightly with oil. Cook the filled crepes on the griddle or in the skillet 2 to 3 minutes on each side, until browned and crisp. Or arrange frozen filled crepes on a buttered cookie sheet and bake 12 to 15 minutes in a 425°F. oven, until the edges are brown and the tops are crispy.

Serve the crepes hot with salsa and additional sour cream.

VARIATION

QUICKER VERSION

Make Super-Simple Baked Pancake, page 18. Either fill with the bean mixture and top with additional sour cream or cut the pancake into wedges, put the wedges on plates, and serve the bean mixture, sour cream, and salsa on the side.

PASSOVER APPLE MATZO BREI

MAKES 4 CUPS BATTER, ABOUT TWENTY-FOUR 3-INCH PANCAKES, ENOUGH FOR 8 PORTIONS

I thought I'd invented this idea until I came across a delightful article where Sheila Linton described her mother's matzo brei, which also included apples and what her mother often referred to as her Three Musketeers: sugar, lemon, and vanilla. Serve with sour cream or vanilla yogurt.

5 large eggs
⅓ cup granulated sugar
¼ cup unsalted butter or margarine, melted, or mild olive or
*   vegetable oil*
1 tablespoon vanilla extract
¼ teaspoon salt
5 whole square 6-inch matzos
1 to 2 medium-size Golden Delicious apples
¼ cup freshly squeezed lemon juice
Oil for cooking

GRIDDLE OR LARGE NONSTICK SKILLET

Put the eggs, sugar, fat of choice, vanilla, and salt into a large bowl. Beat with a wire whisk or electric mixer until well blended.

Fill a medium-size bowl with cold water. Stack the matzos and break into rough quarters or pieces small enough to fit into the bowl of water. Dunk the broken matzos in the water for 30 seconds. Pour off the water. Crumble the matzos into very small pieces (almost a paste) and add them to the egg mixture. Stir gently to coat.

Peel, quarter, core, and finely chop enough apple to make no more than 2 cups. Toss the chopped apple with the lemon juice and stir into the matzo mixture.

Heat the griddle or skillet over moderately high heat until it feels hot when you hold your hand directly above it. Lightly grease the griddle. For each pancake, spoon 1 heaping tablespoon batter onto the griddle; pat lightly with the back of a spatula to flatten slightly. Cook 3 to 4 minutes, until the undersides are golden. Adjust the heat if the pancakes are browning too fast. Turn the pancakes over and press lightly to flatten. Cook about 2 minutes longer to brown the second side.

Keep the pancakes warm in a 200°F. oven, on a cookie sheet or plate, loosely covered, up to 1 hour.

VARIATION

RAISIN APPLE MATZO BREI

Add ½ cup golden raisins to the beaten egg mixture. Continue the recipe and cook as directed above.

SPINACH CREPES WITH MUSHROOM RAGOUT

MAKES 2 ¾ CUPS BATTER, 10 TO 12 CREPES,
AND 3 CUPS RAGOUT,
ENOUGH FOR 5 OR 6 PORTIONS

Both the crepes and the ragout can be made well ahead.

*Half a 10-ounce package frozen chopped spinach, thawed, or
⅔ cup cooked fresh spinach*
1 cup all-purpose flour
1 cup milk
2 large eggs
½ cup water
1 teaspoon salt
Mild olive oil for cooking
1 tablespoon butter
Mushroom Ragout (recipe follows)

A CREPE PAN OR NONSTICK SKILLET, 6 ½ TO 7 INCHES ACROSS
THE BOTTOM, AND A 13 × 9-INCH BAKING DISH

To make the crepes: Squeeze as much water as you can
from the spinach. Put the spinach, flour, milk, eggs, water,
and salt into a food processor or blender and process to
make a smooth batter flecked with spinach. Scrape the sides
once or twice.

continued

Follow the directions for making crepes on page 9, using a scant ¼ cup batter for each.

Melt the butter and use about 1 teaspoon to grease the baking dish. Roll the crepes into cylinders with the first-cooked (brownest) side outside. Arrange in the buttered baking dish and brush with the remaining butter. The crepes may now be tightly covered and refrigerated up to 5 days or frozen up to 3 months.

To serve: Heat the oven to 400° F. Bake the crepes uncovered 10 to 12 minutes, until heated through. Serve with Mushroom Ragout spooned over each serving.

MUSHROOM RAGOUT

This has a very rich flavor. Add a pinch of sugar if the tomatoes seem tart. Use white button mushrooms or a mixture of more exotic kinds such as oyster, shiitake, morel, chanterelle, or porcini.

1¼ pounds mushrooms
2 tablespoons butter
½ cup chopped onion, shallots, or scallions
1 cup canned crushed tomatoes
1 teaspoon salt
¼ teaspoon freshly ground pepper

Rinse the mushrooms or wipe clean with a damp cloth. Remove the stems of shiitake mushrooms, if using. Quarter or slice large mushrooms; leave small ones whole. Melt the butter in a 10-inch skillet over moderately high heat. Add the onion, shallots, or scallions, and cook for about 1 minute. Add the mushrooms and cook about 5 minutes, stirring frequently, until they wilt and change color. Stir in the tomatoes, salt, and pepper. Simmer about 5 minutes, until some of the liquid has evaporated. Serve with Spinach Crepes.

LATKES

Good with sour cream and/or Fresh Applesauce, page 123, for supper. Excellent as a side dish.

1 pound all-purpose potatoes
1 small onion (about 2 ounces)
2 large eggs
¼ cup matzo meal or all-purpose flour
1 teaspoon salt
2 tablespoons plus ¼ cup mild olive or vegetable oil

LARGE NONSTICK SKILLET

Peel the potatoes and cut into ½-inch chunks (you will have about 3 cups). Peel and quarter the onion. Put the potatoes and onion in a food processor and process until finely chopped. Add the eggs, matzo meal or flour, salt, and 2 tablespoons oil to the potatoes. Process just until blended.

Heat 2 tablespoons oil in the skillet over moderately high heat for 2 to 3 minutes, until the oil is very hot. For each latke, spoon about 3 tablespoons (a ¼-cup measure three quarters full) batter into the skillet. Cook 3 to 4 minutes, until the undersides are golden brown and crisp. Adjust the heat if the latkes are browning too fast. Turn the latkes over with a slotted pancake turner and cook 2 to 3 minutes longer to brown the second side. Drain the latkes on paper towels, patting the tops with paper towels, too. Repeat with the remaining oil and batter.

Keep the latkes warm in a 200° F. oven on a plate, uncovered to stay crisp, up to 1 hour.

CARROT AND SWEET POTATO PANCAKES

These are good with roast chicken or baked ham but I like to eat them just by themselves. My husband enjoys leftovers (warmed in a skillet) for breakfast.

1 medium-size sweet potato (about 8 ounces)
2 to 3 medium-size carrots (about 8 ounces)
2 large eggs
⅓ cup all-purpose flour
¼ cup mild olive or vegetable oil
2 tablespoons chopped fresh parsley
1 tablespoon granulated sugar
½ teaspoon salt
Oil for cooking, about 2 tablespoons

GRIDDLE OR LARGE SKILLET

Peel the sweet potato and carrots and cut them into ½-inch chunks. You need between 1½ and 1¾ cups of each vegetable.

Put half of each vegetable into a food processor and turn the machine on/off 3 or 4 times until finely chopped. Add the remaining vegetables and turn the machine on/off about

4 times, until the entire mixture is finely chopped.

Add the eggs, flour, oil, parsley, sugar, and salt to the vegetables. Turn the machine on/off 4 or 5 times, until the ingredients are combined.

To make the pancakes: Heat 1 tablespoon oil in the griddle or skillet over moderate heat. For each pancake, drop about 1 tablespoon batter onto the griddle. Cook 2½ to 3 minutes, until the pancakes are browned on the undersides and start to get crisp around the edges. Adjust the heat if the pancakes are browning too fast. Turn the pancakes over, flatten gently with a spatula, and cook about 2 minutes longer to brown the second side. Repeat with the remaining oil and batter.

Keep the pancakes warm in a 200°F. oven on a plate, uncovered to stay crisp, up to 1 hour. Or let cool to room temperature and reheat uncovered on a cookie sheet in a 200°F. oven for about 15 minutes.

VARIATION

CARROT AND PARSNIP PANCAKES

Follow the recipe but use parsnips instead of the sweet potato.

CLAM AND SCALLION
PANCAKES

MAKES 3 CUPS BATTER,
TWENTY-FOUR 3-INCH PANCAKES,
ENOUGH FOR 4 MAIN-DISH PORTIONS,
OR ABOUT 60 SMALL (ONE-BITE) PANCAKES

A good snack with beer or wine and a fine meal when served with a salad. Serve with sour cream or sour cream mixed with the same amount of plain yogurt.

Two 6 ½-ounce cans minced clams, undrained
1 cup Italian-style packaged bread crumbs
4 large eggs
¼ cup minced scallions
1 teaspoon Worcestershire sauce
1 teaspoon minced fresh garlic
½ teaspoon hot pepper sauce
2 tablespoons butter
1 tablespoon vegetable oil

GRIDDLE OR LARGE SKILLET, PREFERABLY NONSTICK

Put the clams, bread crumbs, and eggs into a large bowl. Stir to mix well. Stir in the scallions, Worcestershire sauce, garlic, and hot pepper sauce. Melt the butter and stir about 1 tablespoon into the clam mixture.

Add the oil to the remaining butter. Use this mixture to grease the griddle.

Heat the griddle or skillet over moderately high heat until it feels hot when you hold your hand directly above it. Brush the griddle with some of the butter-oil mixture. For main-dish pancakes, use 1 heaping tablespoon batter; for bite-size pancakes, use 1 heaping teaspoon batter. Cook 1 to 2 minutes, until the undersides are golden brown. Adjust the heat if the pancakes are browning too fast. Turn the pancakes over and cook 1 to 2 minutes longer to brown the second side.

If made ahead (you may refrigerate them up to 3 days), reheat very carefully in a skillet over low heat. Clams turn tough if the pancakes are heated in a microwave or in an oven higher than 190°F.

POTATO, CHIVE, AND BACON
PANCAKES OR WAFFLES

MAKES 2 ¾ CUPS BATTER, TWENTY 3-INCH
PANCAKES, ENOUGH FOR 6 PORTIONS

Great to make when you
have leftover mashed potatoes. These are delicious with
shredded pork barbecue or scrambled eggs.

3 to 5 thin strips of bacon
1 cup all-purpose flour
1 teaspoon baking powder
½ teaspoon baking soda
½ teaspoon salt (¼ teaspoon if using seasoned leftover potatoes)
⅛ teaspoon freshly ground pepper
1½ cups buttermilk or plain yogurt
1 large egg
3 tablespoons mild olive or vegetable oil
¾ cup mashed potatoes
¼ cup snipped fresh chives or thinly sliced scallions
Oil for cooking

GRIDDLE OR LARGE SKILLET, OR WAFFLE IRON

Cook the bacon until crisp in a skillet or microwave oven;
drain on paper towels and crumble.

Food processor method: Put the flour, baking powder,
baking soda, salt, and pepper into a food processor. Process

briefly to mix. Add the buttermilk or yogurt, egg, and oil; process a few seconds to blend well. Scrape down the sides. Add the mashed potatoes, chives or scallions, and crumbled bacon. Turn the machine on/off 6 to 8 times, just until the ingredients are mixed.

By hand: Put the flour, baking powder, baking soda, salt, and pepper into a large bowl. Stir to mix well. Measure the buttermilk or yogurt in a 2-cup glass measure. Add the egg and oil. Beat with a fork or wire whisk to blend well. Stir into the flour mixture. Whisk in the mashed potato, then the chives and bacon.

Pancakes (see page 6): Heat the griddle or skillet over moderate heat until it feels warm when you hold your hand directly above it. Lightly grease the griddle. For each pancake, pour $1/8$ cup (2 tablespoons) batter onto the griddle. Cook 3 to 4 minutes, until bubbles appear on the surface and the undersides are golden brown. Adjust the heat if the pancakes are browning too fast. Turn the pancakes over and cook 1 to 2 minutes longer to brown the second side.

Waffles (see page 8): Heat the waffle iron. Grease it lightly. Pour in the appropriate amount of batter and spread to the edges. Close and cook until the iron will open easily.

Keep warm in a 200°F. oven—pancakes on a plate and loosely covered to keep moist, waffles directly on the oven rack, uncovered, to stay crisp.

DESSERT

BAKED MOCHA
SOUFFLÉ PANCAKE

This is *serious* chocolate. Serve with a small spoonful of whipped cream, or vanilla or coffee frozen yogurt for contrast. Scoop it from the baking dish with a spoon. Or for a more stylish presentation, turn the pancake out. Loosen the edges with a metal spatula, put a large flat plate upside down on top of the baking dish, and turn the plate and baking dish over together. Lift off the baking dish and sprinkle the pancake with confectioners' sugar. Cut into wedges. Leftovers are great cold.

Butter for the baking dish
⅔ cup granulated sugar
⅓ cup unsweetened cocoa powder
¼ cup instant coffee powder or crystals, preferably espresso
3 tablespoons cornstarch
¾ cup milk
4 tablespoons unsalted butter
1 teaspoon vanilla extract
4 large eggs

AN OVENPROOF SKILLET OR ROUND BAKING DISH, 9 TO 10 INCHES ACROSS THE BOTTOM, SIDES AT LEAST 1 INCH HIGH

Check that one rack is in the middle of the oven and heat the oven to 325°F. Butter the skillet or baking dish and sprinkle 1 tablespoon sugar over the bottom.

Put the cocoa, coffee powder, cornstarch, and all but 1 tablespoon of the remaining sugar into a medium-size saucepan. Mix well, then stir in the milk. Stir over moderate heat until the mixture thickens and boils. Boil 1 minute, stirring constantly. Remove from the heat. Add the butter and vanilla, and stir until the butter is melted.

Crack open the eggs, letting the whites fall into a deep narrow bowl. Stir the yolks into the hot chocolate mixture.

At this point you can cover the chocolate mixture by placing a sheet of plastic wrap right on the surface and put the dessert on hold—at room temperature for not more than 2 hours or in the refrigerator (egg whites, too) for up to 24 hours (in which case allow the mixture and the whites to come to room temperature before proceeding).

Beat the egg whites with an electric mixer at high speed until soft peaks form when the beater is lifted. Beat in the remaining 1 tablespoon sugar and continue beating about 2 minutes longer, until the whites are stiff, glossy, and very white. Beat a spoonful of the whites into the chocolate mixture with the electric mixer. Then, with a rubber spatula, gently fold in the remaining whites. Scrape the batter into the prepared skillet or baking dish.

Bake until the pancake is set around the edges but still slightly creamy in the middle, 20 to 25 minutes for a metal skillet, 30 to 35 minutes in a baking dish. Remove from the oven and serve within a few minutes.

BANANA-FILLED CREPES
WITH ESPRESSO SUGAR

MAKES 1 CUP BATTER, 6 TO 8 FILLED CREPES, ENOUGH FOR 4 TO 6 PORTIONS

F or a quicker but equally delicious version, see the variation at the end of the recipe.

CREPES
1/2 cup milk
1 large egg
2 tablespoons mild olive or vegetable oil
1 teaspoon vanilla extract
1/2 cup all-purpose flour
1 tablespoon granulated sugar
1/2 teaspoon ground cinnamon
Few grains of salt

BANANA FILLING
1 1/4 cups regular, reduced-fat, or fat-free sour cream
1/3 cup granulated sugar
4 small or 3 medium-size ripe bananas

ESPRESSO SUGAR
2 tablespoons granulated sugar
1 teaspoon instant espresso powder
1/4 teaspoon ground cinnamon

A NONSTICK SKILLET OR CREPE PAN, 6 1/2 TO 7 INCHES ACROSS THE BOTTOM

Make the crepes first.

Food processor or blender method: Put all the crepe ingredients into a food processor or blender in the order given. Process 30 seconds to 1 minute, scraping down the sides once, to make a smooth batter.

By hand or electric mixer: Put the milk, egg, oil, and vanilla into a medium-size bowl. Beat until smooth with a wire whisk or electric mixer. Beat in the flour, sugar, cinnamon, and salt until smooth.

Follow the directions for making crepes on page 9, using 3 tablespoons batter for each. Crepes may be made ahead and warmed again before filling.

To make the Banana Filling: Mix the sour cream and sugar in a small bowl. Peel the bananas and slice thinly into the bowl. Mix gently. Cover and refrigerate. You can do this up to 24 hours before serving.

To make the Espresso Sugar: Mix all the ingredients in a small dish.

To assemble: Warm serving plates in a 200°F. or lower oven. Spread the plates out on a counter. Put a warm crepe on each plate. Spoon about ½ cup cold Banana Filling onto one half of each crepe; fold the crepe over the filling. Sprinkle with Espresso Sugar and serve.

continued

VARIATION

Instead of making the crepes, prepare Super-Simple Baked Pancake, page 18. While it bakes, prepare the Banana Filling and Espresso Sugar. Cut the baked pancake into wedges and put the wedges on warmed serving plates. Top with the Banana Filling and sprinkle with some of the Espresso Sugar.

BAKED FRENCH PEAR PANCAKE

MAKES 1 LARGE PANCAKE,
ENOUGH FOR 6 TO 8 PORTIONS

Keep a couple of cans of pears on hand so you can enjoy this dessert any day of the year. It is a thick, custardy pancake about 1 inch high. Leftovers make a delicious breakfast. Serve with or without vanilla yogurt.

Two 16-ounce cans pear halves in extra-light syrup
½ cup all-purpose flour
½ cup packed light brown sugar
4 large eggs
2 teaspoons vanilla extract
⅛ teaspoon salt
4 tablespoons unsalted butter
Confectioners' sugar

A CAKE PAN WITH A NONSTICK FINISH, OR A ROUND BAKING DISH OR AN OVENPROOF SKILLET, 9 TO 10 INCHES ACROSS THE BOTTOM, SIDES ABOUT 1½ INCHES HIGH

Check that one rack is in the middle of the oven and heat the oven to 375°F. Put the chosen baking dish in the oven to heat. Thoroughly drain the pears in a strainer set over a measuring cup or bowl. Reserve ¾ cup syrup.

Put the flour, sugar, eggs, vanilla, and salt into a food processor or blender. Process to a smooth, thick batter, scraping the sides once or twice.

continued

Add 3 tablespoons butter and the reserved pear syrup to the batter. Process to incorporate. Put the remaining 1 tablespoon butter into the baking dish to melt and heat 1 to 2 minutes.

Pour the batter into the baking dish. Arrange the pears in the batter. Bake uncovered about 30 minutes, until brown and puffy. Sift a little confectioners' sugar (through a strainer or dredger) over the warm pancake. Serve with a spoon.

BAKED AUSTRIAN APRICOT ALMOND SOUFFLÉ PANCAKE

MAKES 1 LARGE PANCAKE, ENOUGH FOR 6 PORTIONS

Enjoy this comforting dessert after a light soup, or for brunch.

¼ cup heavy or whipping cream, or evaporated milk
¼ cup apricot no-sugar-added preserves
1 tablespoon freshly squeezed lemon juice
6 large eggs
Few grains of salt
⅓ cup granulated sugar
½ teaspoon vanilla extract
¼ teaspoon almond extract
2 tablespoons all-purpose flour
2 tablespoons sliced or slivered almonds

A ROUND CERAMIC OR GLASS BAKING DISH, ABOUT 9 INCHES ACROSS THE BOTTOM, SIDES AT LEAST 1 INCH HIGH. A 9-INCH PIE PLATE WORKS FINE, TOO.

Check that one rack is in the middle of the oven and heat the oven to 450°F.

Pour the cream, preserves, and lemon juice into the ungreased baking dish. Stir to mix. Spread evenly in the dish.

Crack open the eggs, letting the whites fall into a deep narrow bowl. Put 4 of the yolks into a small container. The 2 remaining yolks are not used in this recipe.

continued

Beat the egg whites and salt with an electric mixer at high speed until soft peaks form when the beater is lifted. Continue beating while sprinkling in the sugar, about 1 tablespoon at a time, until the whites are stiff, glossy, and very white.

Drop the 4 yolks and the extracts into the beaten whites, then sprinkle the flour over the surface. Beat at the lowest speed a few seconds, just until the yolks and flour are mixed in.

Pour the egg mixture over the apricot mixture in the baking dish. Sprinkle with the almonds. Put in the oven and turn the temperature control down to 350°F. Bake 35 to 40 minutes, until the top is well-browned and the pancake is no longer liquid in the center. (The pancake will puff up and then fall.)

Cut in wedges and serve from the dish with a spoon.

HAZELNUT PRALINE CREPES

MAKES 2 CUPS BATTER, 8 TO 10 CREPES, ¾ CUP PRALINE FILLING, ENOUGH FOR 8 PORTIONS

These are rich and fabulous. Serve them after a relatively simple and low-fat main course. All the preparation can be done ahead and the dish of crepes baked shortly before serving. The Praline Filling is great with any plain pancake or waffle.

1½ cups untoasted hazelnuts

PRALINE FILLING
½ cup packed light brown sugar
4 tablespoons unsalted butter, at room temperature

CREPES
2 tablespoons granulated sugar
½ cup all-purpose flour
1 tablespoon unsalted butter
¼ teaspoon salt
1 cup milk
1 large egg
½ teaspoon vanilla extract
Oil for cooking

A CREPE PAN OR NONSTICK SKILLET, 6 ½ TO 7 INCHES ACROSS
THE BOTTOM, AND A 13 × 9-INCH BAKING DISH

continued

Heat the oven to 350°F.

Spread the hazelnuts in a baking pan and bake 10 to 15 minutes, shaking the pan once or twice, until the nuts smell toasty and turn light brown. Wrap the nuts in a dish towel and rub to loosen the skins. Pick out the nuts; some skins will adhere and it's fine to use those nuts.

To make the Praline Filling: Process the brown sugar and butter in a food processor until thoroughly mixed. Scrape the sides. Add ½ cup toasted nuts and process briefly until finely chopped. (Tightly covered, the Praline Filling will keep almost indefinitely in the refrigerator.)

To make the crepes: Finely grind the remaining 1 cup toasted hazelnuts with the sugar in a food processor. Add the flour, butter, and salt and process a few seconds to incorporate the butter. Add the milk, egg, and vanilla. Process several seconds to blend well.

Put a clean dish towel on the counter beside the range. Heat the crepe pan or skillet over moderate heat. Lightly grease. Lift the pan off heat. Pour 3 tablespoons batter into the middle of the pan and rotate the pan clockwise until the batter covers the bottom. Fill any holes by spreading on a little extra batter with a spatula; pour out any excess batter. Put the pan back on heat. As soon as the batter is set—it looks matte and is no longer liquid—loosen the edges with a thin-bladed spatula and turn the skillet upside down over the dish towel so the crepe falls out (these crepes are cooked on one side only).

Continue making crepes with the remaining batter, stacking one on top of the other.

To assemble: Heat the oven to 425°F. Have Praline Filling at room temperature. Lightly butter the baking dish. Turn over the entire stack of crepes so the unbrowned sides are up. Spread 1 tablespoon Praline Filling over the pale side of each crepe to within about 1 inch of the edges. Roll up the crepes and put into the baking dish in a single layer. (If you wish, cover and refrigerate for up to 5 days, or freeze.) Bake the crepes (no need to thaw), covered, for 10 to 15 minutes, until hot.

WALNUT BROWNIE WAFFLES
WITH ESPRESSO CREAM

MAKES 2 CUPS BATTER,
ENOUGH FOR 2 OR 3 PORTIONS

These are like warm cake-style brownies but much quicker to make. For a very pretty dessert make these in a heart-shaped waffle iron. Arrange 3 hearts on each plate with a small spoonful of plain whipped cream and a few raspberries, or a pool of Raspberry Syrup, page 115.

Two 1-ounce squares unsweetened baking chocolate
5 tablespoons unsalted butter

ESPRESSO CREAM
1 cup heavy or whipping cream
2 teaspoons granulated sugar
1 teaspoon instant coffee powder or crystals, preferably espresso

WAFFLES
½ cup granulated sugar
2 large eggs
1 teaspoon vanilla extract
⅔ cup all-purpose flour
¼ teaspoon baking powder
⅛ teaspoon baking soda
2 tablespoons water
⅔ cup walnuts, chopped fine

WAFFLE IRON

Melt the chocolate and butter in a microwave-safe container for about 1 ½ minutes at full power. Stir to blend. Or melt the chocolate and butter in the top of a double boiler over simmering water. Remove from the heat. Let cool slightly.

Meanwhile, mix the Espresso Cream ingredients in a medium-size bowl. Refrigerate about 5 minutes while the coffee dissolves.

In a medium-size bowl, beat the sugar, eggs, and vanilla with a wire whisk or electric mixer to blend well. Whisk in the chocolate mixture, then the flour, baking powder, baking soda, and water. When well blended, stir in the chopped nuts.

Heat the waffle iron (see page 8) on medium if there's a choice. Grease the iron lightly. Pour in the appropriate amount of batter and spread to the edges (the batter is very thick). Close and cook until the iron will open easily.

Keep the waffles warm in a 200°F. oven, directly on the oven rack, uncovered to stay crisp.

While the waffles cook, whip the cream with an electric mixer or rotary beater until soft peaks form when the beater is lifted.

Serve the waffles hot with the cold Espresso Cream.

GINGERBREAD PANCAKES

MAKES 3 CUPS BATTER,
TWENTY-TWO 3-INCH PANCAKES,
ENOUGH FOR 5 TO 7 PORTIONS

Good with vanilla ice cream or frozen yogurt, and/or hot Fresh Applesauce, page 123, or Lemon Sauce, page 119. For a holiday breakfast, serve with Honey Butter, page 127.

1⅓ cups all-purpose flour
1 teaspoon baking powder
½ teaspoon baking soda
¼ teaspoon salt
2 teaspoons ground ginger
1 teaspoon ground cinnamon
¼ teaspoon ground cloves
1 cup buttermilk or plain yogurt
½ cup molasses (not blackstrap)
¼ cup packed dark brown sugar
3 tablespoons mild olive or vegetable oil
1 large egg
Oil for cooking

GRIDDLE OR LARGE NONSTICK SKILLET

Put the flour, baking powder, baking soda, salt, and spices into a large bowl. Stir to mix well.

Measure the buttermilk or yogurt in a 2-cup glass measure. Add the molasses, brown sugar, oil, and egg to the measuring cup. Beat with a fork or wire whisk to blend well. Pour into the flour mixture and stir until well blended.

To make pancakes (see page 6): Heat the griddle or skillet over moderate heat until it feels hot when you hold your hand directly above it. Lightly grease the griddle. For each pancake, pour $\frac{1}{8}$ cup (2 tablespoons) batter onto the griddle. Cook about 1 minute, until small bubbles appear around the edges and the undersides are golden brown. Adjust the heat if the pancakes are browning too fast. Turn the pancakes over and cook about 1 minute longer to brown the second side.

Keep the pancakes warm in a 200°F. oven on a plate, loosely covered to stay moist.

CREPE TORTE

This dessert is unprepossessing but tastes wonderful. It consists of 8 crepes stacked with a thin layer of filling between each. It can be assembled well in advance, then baked at the last minute. Cut it in wedges like a pie. Put the wedges on plates in the kitchen with a tiny scoop of vanilla ice cream (or frozen yogurt) or a small pool of heavy cream alongside.

CREPES
¾ cup milk
1 large egg
2 tablespoons mild olive or vegetable oil
1 teaspoon vanilla extract
½ cup all-purpose flour
2 tablespoons granulated sugar
Few grains of salt

FILLING
½ cup walnuts
3 tablespoons unsalted butter
½ cup apricot preserves
2 tablespoons heavy cream or evaporated milk
Butter for the baking dish

Confectioners' sugar
1 teaspoon butter

A CREPE PAN OR NONSTICK SKILLET, $6^{1}/_{2}$ TO 7 INCHES ACROSS
THE BOTTOM, AND A ROUND BAKING DISH, ABOUT 9 INCHES
ACROSS THE BOTTOM

To make the crepes: Put the milk, egg, oil, and vanilla into a
food processor or blender. Process briefly to blend well. Add
the flour, sugar, and salt. Process to make a smooth thin batter, stopping the machine and scraping the sides once or
twice.

Follow the directions for making crepes on page 9, using 3
tablespoons batter for each.

To make the filling: Grind the walnuts in a food processor
or blender. Melt the butter in a small saucepan over low
heat. Stir the ground walnuts, preserves, and cream or
evaporated milk into the butter and remove from the heat.

To assemble: Butter the baking dish. Place one crepe in
the dish. Spread the crepe with 2 tablespoons filling. Put
another crepe on top. Continue the layers until all the crepes
are used, finishing with a crepe.

Sift 1 to 2 tablespoons confectioners' sugar (through a
small strainer or dredger) over the top. Cut the 1 teaspoon
butter in tiny pieces and scatter them over the sugar. At this
point you may wrap the dessert and refrigerate overnight, or
freeze for up to 1 month. To serve, heat the oven to 400°F.
Bake the torte uncovered for 15 minutes (20 if frozen), until
very hot. Cool to lukewarm and cut into wedges to serve.

ICELANDIC LEMON CREPES

MAKES 2 CUPS BATTER, 10 TO 12 CREPES, ENOUGH FOR 5 PORTIONS

When I was served these by an Icelandic family in Minnesota, they brought back memories of my own childhood in England where they were a favorite dessert. In Iceland and other Scandinavian countries, these pancakes (sometimes spread with strawberry jam and topped with a smidgen of whipped cream) are often served at coffee or tea time.

1 or 2 lemons
2 tablespoons plus ¼ cup granulated sugar
1 cup milk
2 large eggs
2 tablespoons unsalted butter or mild olive oil
1 teaspoon vanilla extract
Few grains of salt
¾ cup all-purpose flour
Oil for cooking
1 tablespoon unsalted butter, cut in tiny pieces

A CREPE PAN OR NONSTICK SKILLET, 6 ½ TO 7 INCHES ACROSS THE BOTTOM, AND TWO 13 × 9-INCH BAKING DISHES

Remove a strip of peel about 2 inches long from one lemon with a vegetable peeler. Squeeze the lemon(s) to make ¼ cup juice; reserve the juice. Put the peel into a food processor or blender along with the 2 tablespoons sugar.

Process 3 minutes (no less), until the peel is chopped as fine as possible, scraping the sides and top once. The sugar will be quite damp.

Add the milk, eggs, 2 tablespoons butter or oil, vanilla, and salt to the sugar mixture. Process a few seconds to blend. Add the flour and process again, stopping the machine once or twice to scrape down the sides, until a smooth batter forms.

Follow the directions for making crepes on page 9, using 2 ½ to 3 tablespoons batter for each. Crepes may be refrigerated for up to 1 week or frozen. If frozen, thaw before continuing on to the next step.

Heat the oven to 425°F. Butter the baking dishes. Fold each crepe in half. Arrange 5 or 6 in each prepared baking dish so they barely overlap. Sprinkle the crepes with the reserved ¼ cup lemon juice and the remaining ¼ cup sugar. Dot with the 1 tablespoon butter.

Bake the crepes uncovered 10 to 15 minutes, until very hot and slightly crisp around the edges. Serve hot or at room temperature.

RUM RAISIN PANNEKUCHEN

MAKES 1 PANCAKE,
ENOUGH FOR 4 TO 6 PORTIONS

In German, *Panne* means "pan" and *Kuchen* means "cake." In any language this is a delicious and very simple dessert—moist bursts of raisins in a creamy base. Try it after a main-dish soup or for Sunday supper. The batter can be made ahead and the dessert baked while the main course is being eaten.

⅓ cup golden raisins
3 tablespoons dark rum
⅔ cup milk
2 large eggs
3 tablespoons granulated sugar
½ teaspoon vanilla extract
⅛ teaspoon salt
½ cup all-purpose flour
1 tablespoon butter
Confectioners' sugar

A 9 ½ TO 10 × 2-INCH QUICHE DISH OR OVENPROOF SKILLET

Check that one rack is in the middle of the oven and heat the oven to 400°F. Put the raisins and rum in a small saucepan or in a microwave-safe dish. Heat 5 minutes over very low heat, or cover and microwave 40 seconds at full power. Let cool until ready to use.

Put the milk, eggs, sugar, vanilla, and salt into a medium-size bowl (or into a food processor or blender). Beat with an electric mixer or wire whisk (or process a few seconds) to blend well.

Add the flour to the milk mixture. Beat (or process) until the batter is very smooth. Stir in the raisins and rum (or turn the processor or blender on/off once).(The batter may stand at room temperature up to 2 hours or be refrigerated up to 24 hours. Stir before using.)

Put the butter in the quiche dish or skillet and melt in the oven 3 to 5 minutes. (The butter must be bubbling hot.)

Pour the batter into the hot butter in the baking dish. Bake uncovered for about 18 minutes (25 to 30 if very cold), until puffed and lightly browned.

Sift (through a strainer or dredger) about 1 tablespoon confectioners' sugar over the pancake and serve hot.

BAKED APPLE WALNUT BLINTZES

MAKES 2¼ CUPS BATTER, ABOUT 14 FILLED CREPES, 3 CUPS FILLING, ENOUGH FOR 7 PORTIONS

These crepes, stuffed with cinnamon-scented apples and then baked, can be filled at least 3 days ahead. Cover and refrigerate or freeze. Do not defrost; simply allow a few additional minutes baking time. Serve as a hearty dessert after a light soup main dish. They are also delicious for Sunday brunch.

1¼ cups milk
1 cup all-purpose flour
3 large eggs
2 tablespoons mild olive or vegetable oil, or unsalted butter, melted
½ teaspoon granulated sugar
Few grains of salt
Oil for cooking
2 tablespoons unsalted butter
Apple Walnut Filling (recipe follows)

A CREPE PAN OR NONSTICK SKILLET, 6 ½ TO 7 INCHES ACROSS THE BOTTOM, AND A BAKING DISH 11 × 7 INCHES OR LARGER

Put the milk, flour, eggs, oil or melted butter, sugar, and salt into a food processor or blender and process to make a smooth batter.

To make crepes for blintzes: Put a clean dish towel on the counter beside the range. Heat the crepe pan or skillet over moderate heat. Lightly grease the pan. Lift the pan off heat. Pour 3 tablespoons batter into the middle of the pan and rotate the pan clockwise until the batter covers the bottom. Fill any holes by spreading on a little extra batter with a spatula. Put the pan back on heat. As soon as the crepe is cooked around the edges and just curling back from the pan, loosen the edges with a thin-bladed spatula and turn the skillet upside down over the dish towel so the crepe falls out. (Yes, these crepes are cooked on one side only.)

Continue making the crepes with the remaining batter (for a total of about 14), stacking one on top of the other.

When you're ready to fill the crepes, melt the 2 tablespoons butter. Brush some on the bottom and sides of the baking dish.

Turn over the entire stack of crepes so the unbrowned sides are up. Lay 4 or more crepes out on the counter top (brown sides down). Put a heaping tablespoon of Apple Walnut Filling on each crepe close to the edge nearest you. Fold the bottom of the crepe over the filling, fold the sides in, then roll the crepe up. Put seam side down in the prepared baking dish. Continue with the remaining crepes and filling. Brush the filled crepes with the remaining melted butter. If you wish, cover and refrigerate up to 3 days or freeze up to 1 month.

To serve, heat the oven to 425°F. Bake the blintzes uncovered 20 to 25 minutes, until browned, slightly crisp, and very hot.

continued

Apple Walnut Filling

This can be made up to 3 days ahead. If you make the filling with a sweet apple, such as Golden Delicious, reduce the sugar to $1/4$ cup.

1¼–1½ pounds (2 large) tart apples, such as Granny Smith,
  Jonathan, Greening, or Braeburn
2 tablespoons frozen apple juice concentrate or unsalted butter
½ cup Zante currants or raisins
⅓ cup granulated sugar
½ teaspoon ground cinnamon
¾ cup walnuts, chopped coarse

Peel, quarter, and core the apples. To chop each quarter quickly: Cut lengthwise in ⅛- to ¼-inch slices, keeping the slices together. Turn the sliced quarter onto its other face and cut lengthwise again (so now you have apple matchsticks). Cut across the matchsticks, making diced apple.

Heat the apple juice concentrate or melt the butter over moderate heat in a 10-inch skillet that has a lid. Add the apples, currants or raisins, sugar, and cinnamon to the pan. Toss gently to mix. Cover and cook 3 minutes, until the apples are tender but still hold their shape. Remove from heat. Stir in the walnuts and cool 5 to 10 minutes before using.

MELTING LEMON PANCAKES

MAKES 3 CUPS BATTER, ABOUT THIRTY 3-INCH PANCAKES, ENOUGH FOR UP TO 10 PORTIONS

Arrange 3 of these small pancakes on a dessert plate with fresh strawberries, raspberries, or blueberries—whatever you can rustle up—alongside. The pancakes are soft and a little tricky to manage (if you're in a hurry, please choose another recipe). Cook them on a nonstick griddle or in a shallow skillet over moderately low heat. Use a thin metal spatula or pancake turner to turn them (not a thick plastic one). They freeze well.

1 or 2 lemons
½ cup granulated sugar
1¼ cups creamed small curd cottage cheese (2% or more milkfat)
⅓ cup uncooked quick (not instant) farina (breakfast cereal)
⅓ cup all-purpose flour
4 tablespoons unsalted butter, at room temperature
2 large eggs
½ cup golden raisins
Oil for cooking
Confectioners' sugar

LARGE NONSTICK GRIDDLE OR SKILLET

Remove 4 lengthwise strips of peel from one lemon with a vegetable peeler.

continued

Put the lemon peel strips in a food processor along with all but about 2 tablespoons sugar. Process 2 minutes, until the peel is very finely chopped (the sugar will look moist).

Squeeze the lemon(s) to make 3 tablespoons juice. Add to the sugar mixture along with the cottage cheese, farina, flour, and butter. Crack open the eggs, letting the whites fall into a deep narrow bowl and adding the yolks to the processor. Process the ingredients about 30 seconds, until very smooth, scraping the sides once. Sprinkle the raisins over the surface. Turn the machine on/off twice to partially mix them in.

Beat the egg whites with an electric mixer at high speed until soft peaks form when the beater is lifted. Add the remaining sugar and beat 2 or 3 minutes longer, until the whites are stiff, glossy, and very white.

Spread the beaten whites over the top of the yolk mixture, mixing them in slightly as you go. Then turn the machine on/off 2 or 3 times, until no traces of white remain. Scrape the mixture into the bowl the whites were beaten in.

To make the pancakes (see page 6): Heat the griddle or skillet over moderately low heat until it feels warm when you hold your hand directly above it. Grease the griddle very lightly. For each pancake, drop about 1 heaping tablespoon batter onto the griddle and spread into a 2-inch round. Cook 2 to 3 minutes, until the undersides are golden brown. Adjust the heat if the pancakes are browning too fast. Turn the pancakes over and cook 2 to 3 minutes longer to brown the second side.

Keep the pancakes warm in a 200°F. oven on a plate or

cookie sheet, covered to stay moist, for up to 1 hour. Sift (through a strainer or dredger) a little confectioners' sugar over the pancakes before serving. Or refrigerate or freeze, and reheat at 200°F. for 5 or 6 minutes.

VARIATION

MELTING CARAMEL PANCAKES

Omit the lemon, sugar, and raisins in the above recipe. Prepare the batter using ½ cup packed light brown sugar and 1 teaspoon vanilla. Continue as directed.

SYRUPS, SAUCES, AND TOPPINGS

BROWN SUGAR SYRUP

The rich flavor makes any breakfast pancake or waffle even more delicious.

1 pound light brown sugar (2 cups packed)
1 cup water

Mix the sugar and water in a medium-size saucepan. Bring to a boil over moderate heat, stirring once or twice to help the sugar dissolve. Boil 5 minutes. Remove from the heat. Serve warm. Store in refrigerator.

NOTE: If the syrup is stored for several weeks, sugar crystals may form in the bottom of the container. Stand the jar of syrup (uncovered) in a small pan of water and heat over moderately low heat until the crystals dissolve. You can also microwave the syrup (without the pan of water) in a microwave-safe jar, 1 or 2 minutes at a time, until the crystals dissolve.

VARIATIONS

BRANDY SYRUP
Add 1 tablespoon brandy to 1 cup of the Brown Sugar Syrup.

Santa Fe Spiced Syrup

Follow the Brown Sugar Syrup recipe but use $1\frac{1}{4}$ cups water. Add two 3-inch cinnamon sticks, 5 whole cloves, and 1 teaspoon anise seed to the sugar and water. Simmer 10 minutes. Remove from the heat and let cool. Strain and use or store as directed.

FRESH ORANGE SYRUP

2 small to medium-size navel oranges
2 lemons
1¹/₂ cups granulated sugar
¹/₄ cup frozen concentrated orange juice plus ¹/₄ cup water, or
   ¹/₂ cup orange juice
One 3-inch cinnamon stick
2 tablespoons Grand Marnier or other orange-flavored liqueur
   (optional)

Remove the peel from one of the oranges and half a lemon with a vegetable peeler. Squeeze the lemons to make ¹/₃ cup juice. Put the citrus peels into a medium-size saucepan along with the sugar, orange juice, and lemon juice.

Add the cinnamon stick and bring to a simmer over moderately high heat, stirring several times to help the sugar dissolve. (Watch carefully; the syrup has a tendency to boil over.)

Reduce the heat to low and simmer 15 minutes. The syrup will thicken slightly. Remove the pan from the heat. Pour the syrup through a strainer. Let cool 10 minutes.

Meanwhile, peel the orange with a serrated knife, removing all the white pith. Working over a bowl or cup measure (to catch the juice), cut out the sections of orange from between the membrane dividers until you're left with just a handful of membrane. Squeeze the membranes over the sections to extract any remaining juice. Cut the sections into small pieces. (You'll have about $^2/_3$ cup cut-up orange; a little more or less will make no difference.)

Add the orange sections and juice to the syrup. Stir in the Grand Marnier or other liquer (if desired). Serve warm or cool. The syrup keeps at least a week in the refrigerator.

BLUEBERRY SAUCE

MAKES 2½ TO 3 CUPS

 For the best flavor, use fresh or frozen tiny "wild" berries when available.

3 cups fresh or one 12-ounce bag frozen blueberries
One 12-ounce jar (1 cup) damson plum preserves, or a
*   10-ounce jar blueberry spreadable or pourable fruit*

Rinse fresh berries and remove any stems or squashed ones. (Don't rinse frozen berries.)

Melt the preserves in a medium-size saucepan over moderately low heat, stirring to break up any lumps.

Add the berries. Increase the heat and stir until boiling. Reduce the heat and simmer 2 to 3 minutes, until the berries have changed color slightly.

Remove from the heat. Serve warm or chilled. Store in the refrigerator up to 1 month.

HOT CRANBERRY KISSEL

MAKES 2 CUPS

Kissel is a saucelike Russian dessert, usually made with one or more red fruits (berries or plums) and often containing red wine. It is wonderful with pancakes and waffles, and even better with a spoonful of sour cream or yogurt on top. The sauce keeps at least a week in the refrigerator.

1 lemon
³/₄ cup granulated sugar
³/₄ cup water
One 12-ounce bag fresh or frozen cranberries
¹/₈ teaspoon ground cinnamon

Remove 3 lengthwise strips of peel from the lemon with a vegetable peeler. Put the peel into a medium-size saucepan along with the sugar and water. Bring to a boil over moderate heat, stirring once or twice to help the sugar dissolve. Reduce the heat and simmer 5 minutes.

Rinse the cranberries (don't rinse frozen berries), and remove any stems or squashed berries. Add to the pan and when boiling, simmer about 5 minutes until most of the skins have popped. Remove and discard the lemon peel. Dip out about 1 cup of the popped berries and reserve.

Puree the remaining berries and the syrup in a food

processor or blender and put back in the pan. Stir in the cinnamon and the reserved berries. Serve warm.

VARIATION

SUMMER CRANBERRY SAUCE

Make this when cranberries aren't available. In a small saucepan, heat one 16-ounce can whole-berry cranberry sauce, 2 strips lemon peel, and about $1/16$ teaspoon ground cinnamon. Simmer 5 minutes over low heat, stirring often, to develop the flavor. Discard peel. Serve sauce warm. Makes $1\frac{1}{2}$ cups.

RASPBERRY SYRUP

MAKES ABOUT 2 CUPS

Try plain or Rich Belgian-Style Waffles, page 21, topped with poached (or canned) peaches, a spoonful of whipped cream, and this tart-sweet syrup. Or serve with Walnut Brownie Waffles, page 90, and whipped cream. If you have a lavish supply from your garden or can buy jam-quality berries for a reasonable price, use 3 cups fresh raspberries instead of the frozen. The syrup keeps several weeks in the refrigerator.

One 12-ounce bag frozen unsweetened raspberries
$^2/_3$ cup granulated sugar
$^1/_2$ cup red currant or strawberry jelly

Mix all the ingredients in a small, heavy saucepan and bring to a full rolling boil over moderately high heat, stirring several times.

Remove from the heat. Press through a fine strainer with the back of a wooden spoon to remove the seeds. The syrup may be served warm (it will be runny); it thickens on chilling.

FRESH STRAWBERRY SAUCE

MAKES ABOUT 1 ²/₃ CUPS

For the freshest flavor and looks, make this sauce just 30 minutes or so before serving, long enough for the juices to flow but not so long that the berries lose their pristine look. Of course, the sauce tastes just fine when kept for a good deal longer, up to 3 days.

1 pint basket fresh ripe strawberries (about 3 cups)
¹/₃ cup granulated sugar
1 tablespoon freshly squeezed lemon juice

Rinse the berries quickly with cold water and remove the green hulls.

Slice the berries thin and put into a medium-size bowl. Sprinkle with the sugar and stir gently to mix well. Cover and let stand 30 minutes at room temperature, stirring once or twice.

Stir in the lemon juice. Serve soon or cover and refrigerate.

STRAWBERRIES AND CREAM TOPPING

Mark's, the restaurant in the Mark Hotel in New York City, serves this summery cream with hot, crisp waffles. What a way to start the day!

1 pint basket fresh ripe strawberries (about 3 cups)
1 cup heavy or whipping cream
1 tablespoon granulated sugar

Rinse the berries quickly with cold water and remove the green hulls. Put the berries on a plate and mash them thoroughly with a fork.

Pour the cream into a medium-size bowl and beat with an electric mixer at high speed until thick. Add the sugar and continue beating until the beater leaves deep trails in the cream. (Keep moving the beater around the bowl so the cream whips evenly.)

With a rubber spatula, gently stir the mashed berries into the cream. Serve the sauce right away or cover and refrigerate up to 3 days.

THICK DRIED-APRICOT TOPPING

MAKES ABOUT 1 1/4 CUPS

As thick as a preserve, this tart topping is also excellent on slices of pound cake for dessert, or on toast at breakfast. Be sure to use moist dried apricots that are light gold, not dark brown, in color.

1 cup water
1/2 cup granulated sugar
4 ounces dried apricots (about 1 cup)

Bring the water and sugar to a boil in a medium-size saucepan over moderate heat, stirring once or twice to help the sugar dissolve. Let simmer about 3 minutes.

Meanwhile, with scissors or a knife, cut each apricot half into 6 to 8 chunks.

Add the cut-up apricots to the syrup. Cover and simmer 20 minutes over moderately low heat. The apricots will soften and absorb some of the syrup.

Store in the saucepan or a glass jar. The topping keeps almost indefinitely in the refrigerator.

Serve warm or cold.

LEMON SAUCE

This sauce, good with Gingerbread Pancakes, page 92, keeps 2 to 3 weeks in the refrigerator.

2 tablespoons granulated sugar
1 tablespoon cornstarch
½ cup cold water
1 or 2 lemons

Mix the sugar and cornstarch in a small saucepan. Stir in the water. Remove the peel from one lemon with a vegetable peeler, letting the peel fall into the saucepan. Squeeze the lemon(s) to make 3 tablespoons juice.

Stir the cornstarch mixture over moderate heat until it is thick, translucent, and comes to a boil. Boil 1 minute. Remove from the heat and stir in the lemon juice. Pour through a strainer to remove the peel. Serve warm or cold.

BUTTERED RUM AND FRESH PINEAPPLE SAUCE

MAKES ABOUT 2 1/2 CUPS

This is Brown Sugar Syrup, page 108, with pineapple added to it, so if you already have a batch of the syrup on hand you can add it to the hot pineapple. Many markets now sell peeled pineapple in the produce section or cut up at the salad bar. The sauce is excellent with any plain pancake or waffle and a side of bacon or ham.

1 pound light brown sugar (2 cups packed)
1 cup water
1/2 medium-size peeled ripe pineapple, or 8 to 10 ounces cut-up
  peeled pineapple from the salad bar
1 tablespoon unsalted butter
2 tablespoons dark Jamaican or Puerto Rican rum,
  or 1 teaspoon vanilla extract

To make the syrup: Mix the sugar and water in a medium-size saucepan. Bring to a boil over moderate heat, stirring once or twice to help the sugar dissolve. Boil 5 minutes. Remove from the heat. You should have 2 cups.

Meanwhile, core the pineapple and cut into 1/4-inch chunks. You need about 1 1/2 cups.

Melt the butter in a medium-size heavy saucepan over

moderate heat. Add the pineapple and cook $1\frac{1}{2}$ minutes, stirring occasionally, until the pineapple is hot. Add the rum or vanilla and let bubble $1\frac{1}{2}$ to 2 minutes.

Add the Brown Sugar Syrup and bring to a boil. Remove from the heat. Serve warm. The sauce keeps in the refrigerator at least a week.

WHIPPED COTTAGE CHEESE TOPPING

Thick and creamy, excellent with waffles.

One 16-ounce carton low-fat, no-salt-added cottage cheese
¹/₄ cup granulated sugar
¹/₂ teaspoon vanilla extract

Food processor method: Process all the ingredients until as smooth and creamy as possible.

Blender method: Put the sugar, vanilla, and about half the cottage cheese into a blender. Blend to a smooth cream, stopping the machine several times to scrape down the sides. (It can take a while until the mixture is freely swirling around the blades.) Add the remaining cottage cheese, about half at a time, blending smooth after each addition. This topping keeps up to 5 days in the refrigerator.

FRESH APPLESAUCE

MAKES ABOUT 3 CUPS

For the best flavor use a mixture of tart (Granny Smith, Greening) and sweet (Golden Delicious, McIntosh, Ida Red, Paula Red) apples. Make plenty because applesauce keeps well and tastes far superior to store-bought. This is a very quick way to make applesauce as it takes little time to grate apples. It keeps at least 2 weeks in the refrigerator.

1 lemon
5 or 6 medium-size (2¹/₂ to 3 pounds) apples
¹/₂ cup water
Granulated sugar, if needed

Remove a strip of peel about 3 inches long from the lemon with a vegetable peeler. Squeeze the lemon to make 1 tablespoon juice. Wash the apples but don't peel or cut them up. Grate them down to the core on the shred side (large V-shaped cuts) of a 4-sided grater. (Or quarter the apples, core them, and grate in a food processor.)

Put the grated apples into a heavy saucepan along with the water, lemon peel, and juice. Cover and cook over moderately low heat for about 20 minutes, stirring 2 or 3 times. Remove and discard the lemon peel. Taste the applesauce; add sugar and/or more lemon juice if you think it needs them. Serve warm or cold.

SAUTÉED APPLES AND RAISINS

MAKES 1 CUP

This delicious recipe can easily be doubled or even quadrupled.

1 large apple (sweet or tart)
1 tablespoon unsalted butter
2 tablespoons packed dark brown sugar
2 tablespoons water
1 tablespoon golden raisins
Few drops lemon juice, if needed

Peel, quarter, and core the apple. Slice crosswise into ¼-inch-thick slices.

Melt the butter in a small skillet over moderate heat. Add the apple and cook for 4 minutes. Shake the skillet to turn the apple slices over or stir gently. Cook 2 to 3 minutes longer, until the apple is almost tender. Add the sugar, water, and raisins. Bring just to a boil. Remove from the heat. Taste; add lemon juice if needed. Serve the sauce warm, or cover and refrigerate up to 1 week and reheat before serving.

VARIATION

MAPLE-APPLE TOPPING

Follow above recipe but use maple syrup instead of the brown sugar and toasted chopped walnuts instead of the raisins.

CILANTRO SOUR CREAM

MAKES ABOUT ¹/₂ CUP

¹/₂ cup regular or reduced-fat sour cream
3 tablespoons minced fresh cilantro leaves
1 tablespoon thinly sliced scallion

Mix all the ingredients. Let stand 30 minutes before using for the flavor to develop. Tightly covered, it keeps 2 to 3 days in the refrigerator.

FRESH TOMATO SALSA

MAKES ABOUT 2 CUPS

1 pound ripe tomatoes
4 scallions
2 very small fresh chilies
¹/₄ cup loosely packed fresh cilantro leaves
1 to 2 tablespoons freshly squeezed lime juice
1 teaspoon salt

Cut out the tomato cores. Cut the tomatoes in half and gently squeeze out the seeds.

By hand: Chop the tomatoes to make about 2 cups. Put into a medium-size bowl. Thinly slice the scallions. Halve, seed, and mince the chilies. Chop the cilantro. Add these to the tomatoes along with the lime juice (to taste) and salt. Stir gently to mix well.

Food processor method: Halve the chilies; remove the seeds. Put in a food processor. Turn the machine on/off until finely minced. Cut the scallions in 1-inch lengths. Add to the processor. Turn the machine on/off for 30 seconds. Add the cilantro; turn on/off 5 or 6 times to chop finely. Add the tomatoes, lime juice, and salt. Turn on/off 6 or 7 times to make a chunky sauce.

Cover the salsa and chill at least 1 hour (or up to 3 days) before serving.

HONEY BUTTER

Make this with regular honey, or with a more exotic honey such as lavender or wildflower. It's a good way to use honey that's too thick to pour for pancakes. Excellent with Old-Fashioned Oat Pancakes, page 16, or any of the basic pancakes. It's really good with the Gingerbread Pancakes, page 92.

8 tablespoons unsalted butter, at room temperature
About 3 tablespoons honey
⅛ teaspoon ground cinnamon

Beat the butter in a small bowl with a wooden spoon or an electric mixer until creamy. Beat in the honey in a stream, scraping the sides of the bowl several times. Beat in the cinnamon. Taste; add more honey if you wish.

Store tightly covered in the refrigerator. It keeps for at least 1 month. Serve at room temperature.

INDEX